Miss Mary Bobo's Boarding House Cookbook

Miss Mary Bobo

Miss Mary Bobo's Boarding House Cookbook

*A celebration of
traditional southern dishes that made
Miss Mary Bobo's an American legend*

Pat Mitchamore
Recipes edited by Lynne Tolley

Rutledge Hill Press®
Nashville, Tennessee
A Thomas Nelson Company

Photographs on pages 30, 72, 87 (left and top right), 92, 96, and 99 © Joe Clark, HBSS.

Photographs on pages 59, 82, 108, 113, 116, 126, 128, 137, 176, and 181 © Junebug Clark.

Published by Rutledge Hill Press, a Thomas Nelson Company, P.O. Box 141000, Nashville, Tennessee 37214.

Typography by Compass Communications, Inc., Nashville, Tennessee
Design by Harriette Bateman

Library of Congress Cataloging-in-Publication Data

Bobo, Mary, 1881–1983.
    Miss Mary Bobo's boarding house cookbook : a celebration of traditional southern dishes that made Miss Mary Bobo's an American legend / [complied by] Pat Mitchamore ; recipes edited by Lynne Tolley.
        p. cm.
    Includes index.
    ISBN 1-55853-314-1
    1. Cookery, American—Southern style. 2. Boardinghouses—Tennessee—Lynchburg—History—20th century. I. Mitchamore, Pat, 1934– . II. Tolley, Lynne, 1950– . III. Title.
TX715.2.S68B62   1994
641.5975—dc20   94-23511
                                                                                                          CIP

Printed in the United States of America

6 7 8—05 04 03 02 01

Contents

Acknowledgments

My sincere thanks go to
Joan Crutcher Ferguson,
granddaughter of Miss Mary Bobo,
for sharing family clippings, letters, photos,
and her own remembrances.
Joan has been an invaluable source of
information. Although much of the history
was available through the Jack Daniel
Distillery files and clips, the personal stories
have enriched the depth and color of the
book. Joan's love of family and Lynchburg
history led her to research available
resources, and she published *Reminiscing
about Lynchburg*, which contains abstracts
from early Lynchburg, Moore County, and
Tennessee newspapers, 1873–1932, in
addition to other clippings and photos. To
assure that this book was historically
correct, Joan allowed me to utilize this
material freely. And for that I am grateful.

Introduction

It is difficult today to imagine a time when we did not have large hotels in exotic places, wayside motels at every interstate exit, and luxurious resorts with lush lawns, rolling golf courses, well-lit tennis courts, and Olympic-sized swimming pools. With room service to bring our food, we hardly need to leave our room, but should we desire to do so, there are often multiple dining rooms on the property. Or, we can just cross the street for our choice of a dozen or so fast-food restaurants.

Since the earliest settlers landed on our shores, the American boarding house was a welcome way of life in each little community. As the country grew and people branched out into the frontier, the boarding house followed. Men who blazed a trail for family and settlers to follow, needed not only housing but also a place to eat. In addition, the isolation of long trails and open spaces created a hunger for companionship.

Today, with the luxury of motel accommodations and restaurants available to us even in many small towns, we find a large segment of our society charmed by wayside inns, bed and breakfasts, and historic, quaint eateries. A fashionable trip now includes at least one stay in an old-fashioned bed and breakfast—room and board! The charm of the past, the simple, unclut-

tered life, no doormen or bellmen, no front desk. Instead, a family's home, all the things that say "make yourself at home" are experienced. What piques our interest and makes us desire this return to yesteryear?

Perhaps it is because our lives are so complicated, but this small glimpse of our heritage gives us a sense of continuity and wholeness. Maybe it helps us appreciate what we have today—and what we had yesterday. Let's face it, the fast foods of burger and fries, fish and fries, or chicken and fries, served in two minutes in paper wrappings to be eaten hurriedly while perched in a plastic-laminated booth, can't begin to satisfy our need for companionship, conversation, comfort, and nurturing (not to mention our desire to be well fed!).

What was a boarding house? Generally, a large house with room to spare, a home to many. First, however, it served as the home to the persons or family that ran the establishment. Second, it was a source of income. In the old days, very few jobs outside the home were available to women. If they were lucky enough to have training, they might pursue employment as nurses or teachers. Otherwise, they worked in a family owned business, such as a store or a boarding house, where they might care for their families while working.

What did a boarding house provide? In

addition to room and board, those who sought shelter in a boarding house were also looking for the creature comforts of home. Traveling businessmen, salesmen, railroad or road workers, vaudeville troupes, bachelors, old maids, and single schoolteachers all needed lodging—and more. Boarding house owners did more than change sheets and cook meals—they provided an extended family. Because all ages of people took room and board, the environment was much like that of a large family sharing one house. Besides the companionship, it afforded security in new surroundings, and it provided a bountiful table with a variety of foods that one person could not achieve.

Food was the one thing that could make or break the reputation of a boarding house. Good food, good reputation!

History of Miss Mary Bobo's Boarding House

In 1908 Lacy Jackson ("Jack") Bobo and his wife, Mary, took over the Salmon House from Dr. E. Y. Salmon and his wife. Dr. Salmon came to Lynchburg, Tennessee, in 1857 to practice medicine. He purchased the house from Thomas Roundtree, a founder of Lynchburg. Mr. Roundtree lived in a log house on the property where the house now stands, prior to building the earlier part of the house. He built the log house in 1818, about the same time that he laid out the town, which was then in Lincoln County. The property on which the house stands was the site of the original lynching tree from which the name Lynchburg is derived. Mr. Roundtree and John Parks had been given license to operate taverns in the area. To attract settlers, Mr. Roundtree also developed several businesses and auctioned off homestead sites.

In 1861, Dr. Salmon left to serve in the Civil War, returning to practice medicine in 1867. At this time he added a large two-story frame residence, attaching it to the original brick structure. A Greek Revival portico gave the house distinction and elegance. The house was Salmon's residence and his place of business. It was known as the Grand Central Hotel and also as the Salmon House and was reputed to be one of the best boarding houses in the region because of its delicious food.

After Dr. Salmon's retirement in 1908, Jack and Mary Bobo acquired the boarding house and changed the name to the Bobo Hotel. They leased the house until Dr. Salmon's death in 1914, when they purchased the property. The Bobos continued the reputation as an excellent boarding house and furthered the reputation of outstanding food, so that now it has become one of the town's permanent fixtures, both socially and commercially.

Over the years Jack Bobo also had a number of other businesses in town. Jack died in 1948 and Mary continued to run the boarding house until her death in 1983, just one month shy of her 102nd birthday. Miss Mary cared for herself, planned the meals, ordered groceries, oversaw the kitchen, managed the staff, and paid the bills until she was 98. She wrote some interesting facts about her life and the boarding house in these later years, which are shared throughout this book.

A few years before she died, Miss Mary stopped taking roomers and began serving mid-day dinner only. Her food was typical

One-half block off the town square is Miss Mary Bobo's Boarding House, sitting very stately, slightly off center, between two old sugar maple trees. For more than a century this house has been a landmark of social and commercial business in Lynchburg, Tennessee. In 1994, Miss Mary Bobo's Boarding House was placed on the National Historic Register.

boarding house fare: simple, abundant, and delicious.

During Miss Mary's final years, the Jack Daniel Distillery sent guests to enjoy meals at the boarding house. By all accounts, everyone was charmed with this old-fashioned experience. Miss Mary continued with her private table, and most every day her daughter and son, also widowed, ate with her. When she died, her children were in their retirement years. It looked like the boarding house would close. However, the Jack Daniel Distillery, interested in the preservation of tradition, realized how important this place was to the town. People they had sent to dine at Miss Mary Bobo's had been raving about the food for years. The distillery purchased the establishment from the heirs and so it continues today as a restaurant.

The boarding house reopened on May 1, 1984, with Lynne Tolley as proprietress. It had been more than seventy-five years since someone other than Miss Mary had run the boarding house.

Lynne Tolley, a fourth-generation Lynchburg native whose family had been distillers with the Tolley and Eaton Distillery, was working for Jack Daniel's in the Nashville office. A great-grandniece of Jack Daniel, Lynne had a degree in home economics. She had eaten at the boarding house many times and had known Miss Mary all of her life. The distillery considered her to be the perfect hostess to fill Miss Mary's shoes. It has proven to be a wise decision.

As promotions manager for Jack Daniel's, I was responsible for special promotions. As executive director and producer of the Mr. Jack Daniel's Original Silver Cornet Band, a national touring show, I promoted goodwill for the brand and for Lynchburg through television, music, and entertainment. The boarding house became a special

This is a copy of the ad that ran in New York Magazine *to promote the tribute to Miss Mary Bobo's Boarding House that the American Festival Cafe at Rockefeller Center held by serving her traditional boarding house dinner. It was such a success that the restaurant extended it for two additional weeks, which proves that meatloaf, country-fried steak, okra, and biscuits are winners even with big city folk!*

promotion and my responsibility there was to promote goodwill through food and hospitality. For the past ten years I have worked to promote Miss Mary Bobo's as a restaurant offering a unique dining experience, and Lynne Tolley as proprietress of this establishment and as an ambassador of goodwill for the brand.

Employing the same cooks and preparing the same recipes, the establishment grew from four dining rooms to five. Mid-day dinner (by reservation only) now has two seatings daily. Each table is cared for by a Lynchburg hostess, ladies from the town who see to it that the bowls and platters are kept full, that everyone meets each other at the table, that the conversation is always flowing, and that everyone has a grand time. The dinner bell is rung for each seating, and guests' names are called as diners follow their hostesses to the dining tables. The hot bowls of food are placed randomly on the long tables. Two entrees are served each day, such as fried chicken, meat loaf, country ham, roast beef, or Miss Mary's Famous Chicken and Pastry. A large variety of vegetables, picked fresh each morning from the two gardens out back, are prepared in true southern tradition and tempt even the most discerning dieter to try just a taste! Fragrant hot bread, rolls, or the southern favorite, cornbread, are made fresh for each meal. This is not a meal for counting out calories. This is an old-fashioned meal worthy of savoring. It is dinner, served as always in the country, at mid-day ("supper" being the lighter evening meal).

Miss Mary Bobo's Boarding House has been honored many times over the years, and history and food have been preserved by its tradition. By sending Lynne Tolley into foreign countries as a Goodwill Ambassador, fame was launched internationally and each week visitors from all over the world come to eat at Miss Mary Bobo's. Three cookbooks have preceded this one,

and visitors from around the world have written to say how much they enjoy them. Although Miss Mary never allowed drinking in her home—nor did she cook with spirits—we found that adding Jack Daniel's Whiskey as an ingredient adds a unique and distinct flavor to many foods. The cookbooks share many of these recipes, and today at least one dish on Miss Mary's table is flavored by the hometown product, Jack Daniel's, adding a unique and flavorful taste experience. In promoting the cookbooks, Lynne and I have both traveled coast to coast stirring up fun and foods from Miss Mary's in cooking schools, celebrity kitchens, and on television talk shows. Special happenings and events and presentations of the boarding house meals have been enjoyed from New York to Chile; from the "Today Show" to "The Home Show"; from Rockefeller Center to the White House.

Family meals, those times when the family gathers together to eat and share their activities of the day, have almost disappeared in today's swarm of conflicting schedules, microwaves, and eating in front of the television. Such fragmentation, however, opened many opportunities to promote a way of life almost forgotten. The tradition begun by Miss Mary now has a future. And a whole new generation has discovered this unique approach to dining. Introducing the experience has been a lot of fun, and because of my work, I have included a taste of the various events offered by my promotions—via photos, menus, or invitations—that have honored Miss Mary, her boarding house, or the foods that are served there.

This cookbook shares Miss Mary's recipes —good, wholesome, nourishing, delicious food. None are difficult to prepare, but all are best when prepared by caring hands and served with friendship—a recipe that all boarding houses—good boarding houses, that is, like Miss Mary's—have found to be foolproof!

On May 1, 1984, Miss Mary Bobo's Boarding House reopened its doors, this time as a restaurant serving mid-day dinner by reservation only. The boarding house, which Miss Mary ran from 1908 until her death in 1983, is owned by the Jack Daniel Distillery. Lynne Tolley, proprietress, continues the fine tradition of southern cooking. Today you can taste some of the delightful dishes flavored with Lynchburg's famous hometown product, Jack Daniel's, a no-no in Miss Mary's day.

Miss Mary Bobo's Boarding House Cookbook

Beverages

Mimosa Punch

2 3-ounce packages strawberry gelatin
2 cups boiling water
1½ cups sugar
2 cups cold water
1 3-ounce can frozen orange juice concentrate
1 46-ounce can pineapple juice
1 cup lemon juice
Large ice ring
2 quarts orange sherbet
1 liter bottle ginger ale, chilled

In a large punch bowl dissolve the gelatin in boiling water. Add the sugar and dissolve completely by stirring. Add cold water. Add the juice concentrate and the remaining juices, stirring to blend. Chill by adding the large ice ring. Before serving, scoop sherbet into the punch bowl and add the ginger ale.
Yield: 40 servings.

Dreamsicle Punch

1 12-ounce can frozen orange juice concentrate
2 cups cold water
1 quart vanilla ice cream
½ gallon orange sherbet
1 liter bottle ginger ale, chilled

In a large pitcher combine the concentrate and cold water and stir to dissolve the juice. At serving time, place the ice cream and sherbet in a large punch bowl, breaking them into large chunks with a spoon. Pour the orange juice over, stirring gently to melt the ice cream and sherbet. Pour the ginger ale over all. More ginger ale may be added as the ice cream and sherbet melt to make additional servings.
Yield: 42 servings.

Bride's Punch

1 12-ounce can frozen lemonade concentrate
1½ quarts water
1½ cups sugar
2 quarts white grape juice, chilled
Large ice ring with lemon slices and mint leaves
1 liter bottle ginger ale, chilled

In a large punch bowl combine the lemonade concentrate and water. Add the sugar and stir until dissolved. Add the grape juice. Chill by adding the ice ring. Add the ginger ale just before serving.
Yield: 24 servings.

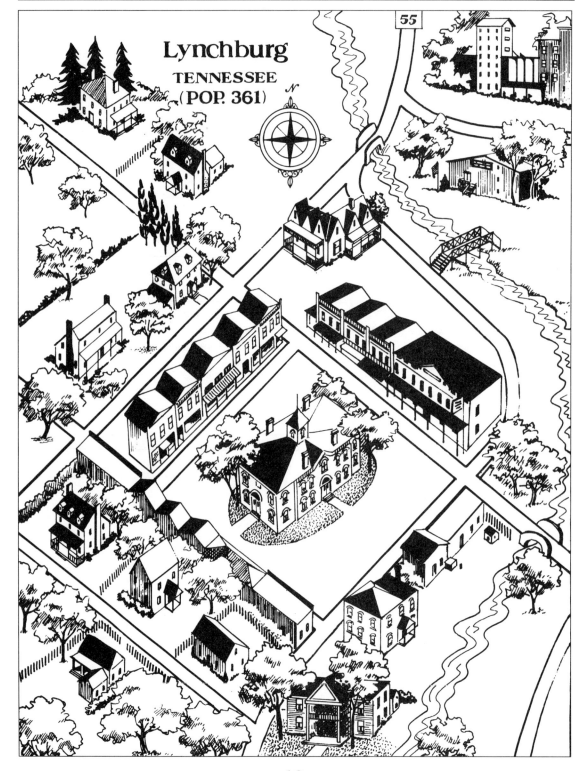

Lawn Party Punch

3 cups sugar
3 cups water
1 46-ounce can pineapple juice
1 12-ounce can frozen orange juice concentrate
1 12-ounce can frozen lemonade concentrate
Large ice ring or cracked ice
1 liter bottle ginger ale, chilled

In a large saucepan combine the sugar and water to form a syrup. Bring the mixture to a boil over medium-high heat. Boil for 7 minutes. Set the pan aside to cool.

In a large punch bowl combine the syrup, pineapple juice, and orange juice and lemonade concentrates. Chill by adding a large ice ring (or cracked ice). At serving time add the chilled ginger ale.
Yield: 25 servings.

Front Porch Punch

Find a cool spot on your porch to sit and enjoy the afternoon! With the pitcher close by and extra glasses, you are sure to attract a gathering of neighbors to sit and chat a spell.

2 3-ounce packages strawberry gelatin
2 cups boiling water
3 cups sugar
Juice of 18 lemons, chilled
1 46-ounce can pineapple juice, chilled
1 quart bottle ginger ale, chilled

In a large pitcher combine the gelatin and the boiling water. Add the sugar and stir until the granules are completely dissolved and the mixture has cooled slightly. Add the chilled juices and ginger ale. Serve over crushed ice in tall glasses.
Yield: 15 to 18 servings.

Down in the Holler Spiced Tea

¾ cup sugar
½ cup instant tea
2 cups instant powdered orange drink
1 2-quart package presweetened lemonade mix
1 teaspoon ground cinnamon
½ teaspoon ground cloves
¼ teaspoon nutmeg

In a large mixing bowl combine all ingredients. Stir to blend well. Store in a tightly closed container. For each cup of tea use two (or more) teaspoons of mix per cup of hot water.

Hot Candied Apple Punch

Delicious! And deliciously fragrant!

2 gallons apple cider (or apple juice)
1 cup cinnamon red hot candies

In a 32-cup percolator place the apple cider. Place the candies in the coffee basket. Perk as for coffee.
Yield: 32 servings.

Mary Evans with her sister, Ophelia, and their half-brother, Frank

From Miss Mary's memoirs: "My father had been married before to Julia Waggoner. They had a son named Frank, who was six years older than me. Julia died and then he married my mother, Susan Birdie Parks. My father and Uncle Newt Parks owned a saloon in town. He had men to run the farm. He rode a large yellow horse back and forth to work. They kept a white woman to help care for us and the work.

"My mother used to tell us when she was a little girl during the Civil War, how they would hear the soldiers tramping and run and hide. Being a rich agricultural district, it was constantly being preyed upon by foraging parties sent out from the army stationed at near points. They had to live in constant fear of bushwhackers and raiding parties."

Photo courtesy of Joan Crutcher Ferguson

Everybody's Treat

1 quart sherbet, any flavor, softened slightly
3 cups buttermilk
Fruit for garnish

In a large bowl place the sherbet and buttermilk. With a mixer on low speed gently mix until slushy. Pour into tall slim soda glasses, garnish with pieces of fruit (lime wedge for lime sherbet, pineapple wedge for pineapple, etc.) and a straw. Delicious!
Yield: 8 servings.

Southern Iced Tea

1½ cups water
5 regular-size tea bags, orange pekoe and black pekoe tea
1¼ cups sugar
Lemon wedges

In a small saucepan bring the water to a boil. Add the tea bags and allow to boil for one minute. While the tea is boiling measure the sugar into a 2-quart pitcher. Remove the tea and add another cup of water to it to cool the tea somewhat before pouring it over the sugar, stirring well to dissolve the sugar. Keep filling the saucepan with water (this rinses the leaves) and add to pitcher until filled.

To serve, pour into glasses filled with ice. Garnish with a lemon wedge. Something wonderful!
Yield: 8 servings.

Rich Hot Chocolate

1½ cups sugar
½ cup cocoa
Dash salt
5 cups water
1 13-ounce can evaporated milk
2 cups milk
Marshmallows or whipped cream

In a large saucepan stir the sugar, cocoa, and salt together. Slowly add the water and bring the mixture to a boil. Add the milk and heat until thoroughly warm. Serve in mugs topped with marshmallows or whipped cream.

Note: Adults may add Jack Daniel's Whiskey to their hot chocolate for a rich Tennessee Mud!
Yield: 12 servings.

Sweet Eye Opener

1½ quarts apple cider
2 12-ounce cans apricot nectar
1½ cups orange juice
¾ cup lemon juice

In a larger pitcher combine all of the ingredients. Cover and chill thoroughly. Serve for breakfast in juice glasses or over ice.
Yield: 12 servings.

Ervin Crutcher's Egg Nog

6 eggs, separated
1½ cups sugar, divided
1½ cups Jack Daniel's Whiskey
1 pint whipping cream
1 cup milk
Grated nutmeg

In a medium bowl beat the egg whites until stiff. Gradually beat in ½ cup of sugar until the egg whites are glossy, not dry. Set the bowl aside.

In a large bowl beat the egg yolks until thick and yellow. Add the remaining sugar and mix well. Gently pour in the Jack Daniel's Whiskey and mix to blend.

In a small bowl whip the cream until stiff.

Add the egg whites to the egg yolk mixture in the large mixing bowl, folding gently with a spoon to blend. Now gently fold in the whipped cream. Pour or ladle into a large punch bowl. Add the milk and mix gently but thoroughly. Serve in crystal or silver punch cups and top with a sprinkling of grated nutmeg.
Yield: 16 servings.

Boiled Custard

4 cups half-and-half
6 eggs
¾ cup sugar
3 tablespoons all-purpose flour
1 tablespoon vanilla
Nutmeg
Jack Daniel's Whiskey (optional)

In the top of a large double boiler heat the half-and-half until very hot but not boiling. In a medium mixing bowl beat the eggs with an electric mixer until yellow and fluffy. In a separate bowl combine the sugar and flour. Stir the dry ingredients into the eggs and add the vanilla. Carefully add a small amount of the hot half-and-half into the egg mixture, enough to warm the eggs. Pour the egg mixture into the hot half-and-half. Continue to cook over boiling water approximately 25 minutes, stirring constantly until the custard coats a metal spoon and is the consistency of very heavy cream. Remove the pan from the heat and cool.

Pour into crystal punch cups and sprinkle with grated nutmeg. Pass a small silver pitcher of Jack Daniel's Whiskey to those desiring to add some spirit.
Yield: 6 servings.

Holiday Wassail

1 gallon apple cider
2 tablespoons whole allspice
16 whole cloves
1 cinnamon stick
1½ cups sugar

In a large saucepan heat the cider until simmering. Tie the spices in a cheesecloth square and drop into the simmering cider. Stir in the sugar. Simmer for 30 minutes but do not boil. Remove the spices and serve in hot punch cups.
Yield: 20 servings.

HISTORY

A Political Campaign, a Band, and a Parade

*The following article describes an election
year in Lynchburg, with a note from Miss
Mary about her ride in the parade.*

IN THE YEAR 1896, Governor Robert L.
Taylor spoke here in behalf of the
Democratic Party on William Jennings
Bryan's free silver ticket and his own race for
Governor.

The Lynchburg Band met Bob Taylor in
Mulberry followed by a long string of ladies
and gents on horseback. There were many
white horses in the parade.

Mrs. Mary Evans Bobo, Mrs. Lula Bobo
Holt, and Mrs. Pearl Parkes Bobo are the
only ones living today that rode in that
parade seventy years ago.

John Billingsly, the livery stable owner, and
Ben Warren, the blacksmith, rigged up a
band wagon, a hay-frame like, with seats on
the side and the driver's seat mounted higher.
George Berry was the driver and the flag was
carried by Uncle Jep Austin. All the band
members wore free silver hats, and were
quite handsome.

The parade arrived in Lynchburg about
dark and the town was alive with people to
hear "Our Bob" speak.

Mrs. W. W. Holt was driving the family rig
pulled by a strawberry roan horse. Major H.
B. Morgan and the Taylor Brothers, Captain
Bill, John and Marion and all the 'died in the

wool' Democrats that didn't go to Mulberry,
met the parade at the Jack Daniel ford, two
miles out of town.

This night was long before electric lights,
and the town was aglow with hundreds of
candles. The south and east sides were aglow;
however, the north and west sides were not
as well lighted since there were only four
buildings on the north side, and one of these
was the livery stable.

Tom Holt, a County Line merchant,
brought up the rear of the parade driving a
nice brown mare. He was standing up in the
buggy waving his whip and singing "Away
Over Yonder in the Promised Land."

Bob Taylor spent the night at the Salmon
House, now the Bobo Hotel, and the next
day the band led him over to Flat Creek and
on to Shelbyville. They were met in Shelbyville by other bands, and late in the evening
as each band left the square playing different
numbers, our band was playing "God Be
With You Till We Meet Again."

From Miss Mary's memoirs: "I remember
riding a gray horse to Mulberry to meet Bob
Taylor. I wore a riding habit made out of
brown domestic and it had pearl buttons."

Lynchburg Lemonade

During Miss Mary Bobo's lifetime she never served any strong drink at the boarding house. However, since her death there have been some occasions where this famous drink was served on the porch or front lawn. One such occasion was in 1986, when Tennessee's governor, Lamar Alexander, and author Alex Haley came to Lynchburg to kick off the year-long celebration Home-coming '86. Lynchburg Lemonade was served on the front lawn prior to mid-day dinner at the boarding house. It has been served to other notables on special occasions since that time.

1 part Jack Daniel's Whiskey
1 part Triple Sec
1 part bottled sweet and sour mix
4 parts Sprite
Crushed ice
Lemon slices
Maraschino cherries

In a pitcher combine the first four ingredients. Add ice and stir. Garnish with lemon slices and cherries. Great by the pitcher or by the glass.

Grapefruit Ice

2 cups sugar
2 cups water
2 15-ounce cans crushed pineapple
2 16-ounce cans grapefruit sections
1 16-ounce jar maraschino cherries
1 liter ginger ale

In large saucepan combine water and sugar. Heat until the sugar is dissolved and cool. Meanwhile in a blender or processor, combine crushed pineapple and grapefruit sections and blend until fine. Add cherries and blend for additional minute. Stir in cooled, simple syrup and place in container to freeze until firm. To serve, place in a punch bowl and pour ginger ale over. Tangy and refreshing!
Yield: 24 servings.

Spiced Grape Punch

4 cups grape juice
1 cup sugar
1 6-ounce can frozen lemonade concentrate
1 6-ounce can frozen orange juice concentrate
6 cups water
3 sticks cinnamon sticks, broken into pieces
6 whole cloves

In a large saucepan combine juices, sugar, and water. Tie spices in a small square of cheesecloth and place in pan. Simmer together for 15 minutes. Remove spices and serve hot.

Appetizers

Unforgettable Ham Balls

1 pound ground cooked ham
½ pound ground fresh pork
1½ cups soft bread crumbs (about 3 slices)
2 tablespoons Jack Daniel's Whiskey, divided
2 tablespoons water
1 egg
¼ cup celery, minced
2 tablespoons onion, minced
½ teaspoon dry mustard
¼ teaspoon pepper
⅛ teaspoon ground cloves
⅓ cup firmly packed brown sugar
1 tablespoon prepared mustard
1½ teaspoons vinegar

In a large bowl combine the ham, pork, bread crumbs, 1 tablespoon of Jack Daniel's Whiskey, water, egg, celery, onion, dry mustard, pepper, and cloves. Shape the mixture into meatballs (1 tablespoon each). Arrange the meatballs on a baking sheet. Bake at 350° for 15 minutes or until fully cooked.

In a small saucepan combine the brown sugar, prepared mustard, vinegar, and remaining 1 tablespoon of Jack Daniel's Whiskey. Stir over low heat until hot. Use toothpicks to dip the cooked meatballs in the sauce.
Yield: 20 to 25 meatballs.

Ham and Cheese Appetizer Muffins

¼ cup butter
½ cup onion, minced
¼ cup green bell pepper, minced
1 clove garlic, minced
2 cups all-purpose flour
1 tablespoon baking powder
1 teaspoon salt
½ teaspoon freshly ground pepper
1 cup milk
2 eggs
1 cup ham, finely diced
½ cup Cheddar cheese, cubed
¼ cup sunflower seeds, roasted and shelled

Grease or paper line 36 miniature muffin cups. In a skillet melt the butter and sauté the onion, green pepper, and garlic until the vegetables are tender.

In a large bowl combine the flour, baking powder, salt, and pepper. In a small bowl beat the milk and eggs together. Add the liquid mixture to the dry ingredients along with the vegetable mixture, ham, and cheese. Stir the mixture just until moistened. Spoon into muffin cups. Sprinkle sunflower seeds over the tops. Bake at 375° for 15 to 20 minutes or until a toothpick inserted in the center comes out clean.
Yield: 36 muffins.

**Mary Evans with her younger sister, Ophelia,
later to become the wife of Lem Motlow, heir to the Jack Daniel Distillery**

From Miss Mary's memoirs (dated September 1967): "Ophelia and I both loved the piano. We took lessons from many ladies in the area. We rode to school in a buggy and put the horse in someone's barn. We took our lunch every day. This consisted of ham, sausage, or chicken with a biscuit and a pie or a cake. Ophelia and I wore our hair plaited tight. We wore calico dresses and went barefooted in warm weather. We wore hoods or fascinators on our head. Always wore a pretty blue veil over our faces in the winter. In the summer, the teachers had a two-week institute. They had classes and programs. We went to that too. Ophelia and I both had a part in the spelling match and both won on our side.

"We used to go swimming in the creek in front of the house and that was a good time, had no swimming pools or swim suits. Won't tell you what we wore!"

Photo courtesy of Joan Crutcher Ferguson

Tuxedo Taters

24 very small new potatoes, unpeeled
1 8-ounce carton sour cream
½ package ranch-style salad dressing mix
Paprika

In a large saucepan boil the unpeeled potatoes in water to cover until done but not overcooked. Drain and cool. Scoop out the top portion of the potatoes and mash thoroughly. Add the sour cream and blend. Add the dressing mix and stir well. Place one tablespoon of the mixture into the potato cavities and garnish with paprika. Allow 2 potatoes per person.
Yield: 12 servings.

Sugared Mint Leaves

3 cups mint leaves
1 egg white
Confectioners' sugar

Wash the freshly picked mint leaves in cold water and place on a paper towel to dry. Dust a bread board with sifted confectioners' sugar. Dip each mint leaf in the unbeaten egg white. Next lay the mint leaf on the sugar and tap it lightly, then turn and tap again. Place the coated leaves on a cookie sheet and refrigerate.

These will become as stiff as potato chips. Use to garnish dishes, fruit plates, salads, ice cream, sherbet, or puddings, or eat as a sweet taste-refresher between courses.
Yield: 3 cups.

Front Porch Crackers

Excellent as a snack, appetizer, or accompaniment to a salad at mealtime.

1 cup mayonnaise
¾ cup sharp Cheddar cheese, grated
½ teaspoon dry mustard
½ teaspoon caraway seeds
Ritz crackers
Mayonnaise
1 large onion, finely chopped

In a medium bowl mix together the mayonnaise, cheese, mustard, and caraway seeds. Set aside.

Spread a thin layer of mayonnaise on Ritz crackers. Sprinkle with onion. Place a teaspoon of the cheese mixture on top. Place the crackers on a baking sheet and place under the broiler until hot. Serve immediately.
Yield: 10 servings.

Pineapple Cheese Spread

1 8-ounce package cream cheese, softened
¼ cup chutney
¼ teaspoon dry mustard
3 tablespoons Jack Daniel's Whiskey
1 small pineapple half, cut lengthwise
½ cup almonds, sliced and toasted

In a small bowl blend the cream cheese, chutney, mustard, and Jack Daniel's Whiskey until well mixed. Scoop out the inside of the pineapple half and fill with the cream cheese mixture. Refrigerate. When ready to serve sprinkle almonds over the top and serve with crackers.
Yield: 1½ cups.

Uncle Jack's Red Dogs

These delectable tidbits have been served from sea to shining sea.

1½ cups catsup
¼ cup brown sugar
¼ cup Jack Daniel's Whiskey
1 package cocktail wieners (or hot dogs cut into 1-inch pieces)

In a small saucepan combine the catsup and brown sugar. Heat over low heat until the sugar dissolves. Remove the pan from the heat and add the Jack Daniel's Whiskey. This can be served in a chafing dish with cocktail wieners or used as a sauce over hot dogs in buns. All proportions are approximate. You may adjust to your own taste.
Yield: 24 to 30 servings.

Ridge-Runner Hot Dogs

These are so called because everyone runs fast for refills.

1 12-ounce bottle chili sauce
½ cup grape jelly
½ cup apricot preserves
½ cup Jack Daniel's Whiskey
1 package cocktail wieners (or hot dogs cut into 1-inch pieces)

In a medium saucepan combine the chili sauce, jelly, and preserves. Stir well to blend. Heat over medium low heat until the jelly is melted. Stir in the Jack Daniel's Whiskey and cocktail wieners.

Note: This is also delicious over meatballs. These may be served in a chafing dish.
Yield: 24 to 30 servings.

Chopped Chicken Liver

1 pound chicken livers
4 tablespoons cooking oil, divided
Salt and pepper
1 cup onion, chopped
4 eggs, hard-boiled and chopped
Sour cream

In a medium skillet over high heat, fry the chicken livers in 2 tablespoons of cooking oil for about 3 minutes. Salt and pepper generously. In another smaller skillet saute the onions in remaining oil until golden. In a food processor, combine the livers, onions, and chopped eggs. If the mixture is too dry, add a small amount of sour cream. Place in a mold and refrigerate until serving time.

This can be served with a dollop of sour cream to garnish, or use another hard-boiled egg and parsley. Serve with crackers.
Yield: 8 to 10 servings.

Miss Mary's Mother, Bird Parks Evans

From Miss Mary's memoirs: "Mother was a good Christian woman, belonged to the Methodist Church here in town. She went to Sunday School and Church and took her children. Mother went to Methodist Conference when it was in nearby towns and always took several ladies with her. Mother had tenants on the farm, so after my Papa died (at age 39) mother always managed to make a good living for us. We had cattle, sheep, hogs, mules, and horses. She raised corn, wheat, rye, oats, and hay. We took the wheat to the mill for flour, corn to the mill for meal, and used some to feed the stock. We used the mules for plowing and the wagon. We used the horses to ride and for the buggy. We also had a two seated surrey, which is rare. We milked cows, churned butter, killed hogs, and cured the hams in a large smoke house."

Photo courtesy of Joan Crutcher Ferguson

Tom Motlow

>─┤◄►─○─◄►┤─◄

TOM MOTLOW, nephew of Jack Daniel and younger brother of Lem, who had inherited the distillery, lived at the Bobo Hotel, as it was known at one time, for more than forty years. A bachelor, he enjoyed the food and companionship afforded by such a hospitable residence. His strong opinions were shared in conversation at the table or on the porch after supper. One opinion fueled a feud of sorts with another longtime boarder, Will Parks, owner of the local Ford dealership.

Mr. Tom was staunchly against cars, and especially Fords, because they were the rage and the topic of all conversations. As a banker, he was approached almost daily for car loans. Nothing satisfied him more than to relate at the table that he had refused such a loan that day.

A fad fueled by the Fords was tin lizzie jokes. In fact, there was a fashionable magazine of the period, jayhawked at newsstands and on the railroads, that had nothing but the latest Ford jokes. Poking fun at the cars' peculiarities probably fanned the public's interest even more. However, Will Parks lacked the good humor of the tin lizzie jokes, knowing that the local banker was not sympathetic to car loan applications. Each evening the conversation opened up with the latest Ford joke, such as "A fellow in town just named his Ford after his wife. He said that he did so because he can't control either one." Or, "A Ford is really a family car, there is a hood for Mama, a tank for Papa, and a rattle for Baby."

One evening after supper, when everyone was on the porch enjoying the summer evening, one of the boarders wanted to share the latest Ford joke. Instead of saying "latest," he mistakenly said "last," starting off with "Have you heard the last Ford story?" whereupon Will Parks said, "I certainly hope so." This joke and his retort were remembered long after all the stories were forgotten.

The feud became so heated that for many years Mr. Tom and Will Parks stopped talking to one another. They lived at the boarding house (both men died while still living at the boarding house and each well into his nineties) and took all their meals together at the table but refused to speak to each other. Later Mr. Tom bought a car for himself. Remembering all the Ford jokes and the icy disposition of the Ford dealer, he bought himself a Chevy.

Accompaniments

Tomato Marmalade

When the garden was overflowing with ripening tomatoes, the cooks would often stir up this wonderful condiment to spoon over hot biscuits or cornbread, or to eat with white beans.

6 cups ripe tomatoes, peeled and chopped
l lemon with rind, thinly sliced
6 cups sugar
2 teaspoons ground cinnamon
1 teaspoon ground cloves
½ teaspoon salt

In a large stewing pan bring all of the ingredients to a boil. Simmer over medium heat, stirring and skimming the top occasionally. Cook for about 1 hour or more. The marmalade will thicken. Be careful that it doesn't burn. If necessary adjust the heat and stir more often. Pour into large sterilized jars and allow the marmalade to cool. Store in the refrigerator.

Note: If you wish to can this, refer to your canning directions. Most often these were eaten within a week at the boarding house and therefore could be stored in the refrigerator like other jellies that had been opened.
Yield: 8 cups.

Green Tomato Mincemeat

This delicious condiment was one of Miss Mary's recipes served at the American Festival Cafe in Rockefeller Center during its tribute to Miss Mary Bobo's Boarding House.

4 large green tomatoes, chopped
4 large apples, peeled, cored, and chopped
3 cups light brown sugar, firmly packed
¼ cup butter
3 cups golden raisins
1 teaspoon ground cloves
1 teaspoon ground nutmeg
1 teaspoon ground cinnamon
1 cup apple cider vinegar
1 cup English walnuts, chopped

In a large heavy saucepan combine all of the ingredients except the nuts and simmer for 2 hours or until thickened. Remove the pan from the heat and add walnuts. Allow to cool. Cover and refrigerate.

Note: This is delicious served as an accompaniment to game, ham, or poultry. Or you may add a generous dollop of Jack Daniel's Whiskey and use as a filling for tarts or pies.
Yield: 2½ quarts.

Rebel Raisins

2½ cups raisins
3 tablespoons butter
2 tablespoons all-purpose flour
3 tablespoons brown sugar
2 tablespoons lemon juice

In a heavy saucepan barely cover the raisins with water and bring to a boil. Lower the heat and simmer for 20 minutes or until the water begins to evaporate. Add the butter. In a small bowl stir together the flour and brown sugar. Sprinkle the mixture over the raisins, stirring constantly. Cook until thickened. Add the lemon juice and serve. This is especially good with baked ham!
Yield: 2½ cups.

Glaze for Baked Ham

1 cup orange juice
¼ cup Jack Daniel's Whiskey
½ cup brown sugar
1 tablespoon ground ginger
½ teaspoon whole cloves

In a small saucepan combine all of the ingredients and bring the mixture to a boil. Reduce the heat and simmer for about 30 minutes or until syrup-like in consistency. Brush over ham several times during the last hour of baking.
Yield: 1½ cups.

Easy Corn Relish

1 12-ounce can whole kernel corn
⅓ cup corn liquid
1 small onion, thinly sliced
2 tablespoons bell pepper, chopped
2 tablespoons pimiento, chopped
¼ cup vinegar
½ teaspoon cornstarch
¼ cup light brown sugar
½ teaspoon salt
¼ teaspoon mustard seed
½ teaspoon celery seed
¼ teaspoon red pepper sauce

Drain the liquid from the can of corn, reserving ⅓ cup of liquid. Set the corn aside.
    In a small saucepan combine the reserved liquid with the remaining ingredients. Bring the mixture to a boil, reduce the heat, and simmer for 5 minutes. Remove the pan from the heat. Stir in the reserved corn. Cool and refrigerate.
Yield: 2 cups.

Fast Corn Relish

1 16-ounce can whole kernel corn, well drained
¾ cup chili sauce
1 small onion, finely chopped
2 tablespoons green pepper, finely chopped
1 rib celery, minced
¼ cup sweet pickle relish

Combine all ingredients and stir to blend. Cover and chill before serving.
Yield: 3 cups.

Miz Bobo's Cabbage Relish

2 cups cabbage, finely chopped
1 large red bell pepper, finely chopped
1 large green bell pepper, finely chopped
1 cup celery, finely chopped
4 teaspoons salt
2 tablespoons mustard seed
3 tablespoons brown sugar
1 cup vinegar

In a large bowl toss the cabbage, chopped peppers, and celery with salt. Cover and chill overnight.

Rinse and drain the cabbage mixture in a colander until all the liquid is gone. In a small saucepan combine the mustard seed and brown sugar with vinegar. Bring the mixture to a boil. Pour over the drained vegetables. Chill overnight.
Yield: 3 cups.

Easy Pickled Pears

1 30-ounce can pear halves
Whole cloves
1 cup apple juice
¼ cup apple cider vinegar
½ cup reserved pear juice
1 8-ounce package cinnamon red hot candies

Drain the pears, reserving the juice. Place cloves into each pear half, using three or four per half.

In a medium saucepan, combine the apple juice, vinegar, candies, and ½ cup of reserved pear juice. Bring to a boil to melt the candies. Add the pear halves. Simmer gently for about 5 minutes. Cover and refrigerate until serving time. Arrange on a serving dish and spoon the liquid over the top.

Note: This can also be served as a dessert. Place in dessert dishes and top with a dollop of whipped cream, if desired.
Yield: 6 servings.

Pickled Pigs' Feet

Boiled pigs' feet
Vinegar, heated
Whole cloves
Whole allspice
Black peppercorns

In a large pan cover the pigs' feet with water and boil until tender. Make sure that the water always covers the pigs' feet by one inch during cooking. Remove the pigs' feet and place in a hot sterilized jar; cover with the hot vinegar. For each quart of vinegar add: 8 cloves, ¼ teaspoon of allspice, and ½ teaspoon of peppercorns. Cover and place in the refrigerator. Let them stand for at least 3 days.

Note: These were usually made in gallon jars and kept refrigerated. Southern kitchens always served pickled dishes as relishes and accompaniments to meals. The type served would depend on what was fresh and available. These would be a delicacy and available during hog killing time, or when the first frost happened in the fall of the year.

Miss Mary Evans with Beau during her Courting Days

Miss Mary Evans with her beau, Marvin Kimbro, before her marriage to Lacy Jackson Bobo. The roads were unpaved and dusty and travel was accomplished by horse and buggy. Even traveling a short distance to go courting was more difficult than it is today. However, the open air and dust did not prevent the young couple from dressing formally for the occasion.

Photo courtesy of Joan Crutcher Ferguson

Pepper Vinegar

Pack a vinegar cruet with red cayenne peppers that have been rinsed with water to clean. Do not remove the tops of the peppers. Boil apple cider vinegar and pour enough into the cruet to completely cover the peppers. Add a pinch of canning salt (canning salt has no iodine and prevents vinegar from becoming cloudy). Put a stopper in the cruet and leave for several days. Use for seasoning turnip greens or other vegetables. The mixture will keep for months and does not need to be refrigerated.
Yield: 1 cruet.

Chow Chow

3 pounds green tomatoes, chopped
1 small head cabbage, shredded
2 large sweet onions, chopped
2 red bell peppers, chopped
2 green bell peppers, chopped
3 cups white distilled vinegar
2 cups sugar
2 tablespoons pickling spice
1 tablespoon mustard seed
1 tablespoon salt (not iodized)

In a large enamel or stainless steel pot combine all of the ingredients. Mix well and bring to a boil. Reduce the heat and simmer for 12 minutes, stirring occasionally. Pour into a hot sterilized quart jar; cool and refrigerate.

Note: This is delicious as a side dish with pinto or white beans and cornbread.
Yield: 4 cups.

Red Cocktail Sauce

2 cups thick sweet catsup
¼ cup Worcestershire sauce

In a mixing bowl combine the ingredients and stir to blend. Cover and refrigerate until serving time. This cocktail sauce is excellent for boiled shrimp or fried fish. Store any unused portion in the refrigerator.
Yield: 2¼ cups.

Best Mustard and Horseradish Sauce

1 tablespoon sugar
3 tablespoons mustard
2 tablespoons vinegar
1 tablespoon water
¾ teaspoon salt
2 egg yolks, slightly beaten
1 tablespoon butter
1 tablespoon prepared horseradish
½ cup whipped cream (or non-dairy whipped topping)

In the top of a double boiler, combine the sugar, mustard, vinegar, water, and salt. Stir in the egg yolks to mix well. Cook over hot (not boiling) water for 5 minutes until sauce is thick. Blend in the butter and horseradish. Remove the pan from heat and cool. Whip cream and fold into sauce. Cover and store in the refrigerator. Excellent with roast beef or Salmon Loaf or Mary Lou's Salmon Cakes (see page 98).
Yield: 1 cup.

Breakfast Ham and Biscuits with Red-Eye Gravy

3 slices Tennessee country ham, about ¼ inch
    thick
¼ cup strong coffee
¼ teaspoon sugar
Biscuits (or your favorite bread)

In a large iron skillet fry the ham slices on each side. Remove the ham to a platter. Add the coffee and sugar to the pan drippings in the skillet. Stir to blend over low heat. Cut the ham into 2-inch square pieces and return to the gravy. Simmer just until hot. Place the ham pieces on top of the split biscuits. Spoon one or two teaspoons of red-eye gravy over the top. Serve now, while hot...outstanding!

Note: At the boarding house, Tennessee country ham has always been used, but in other parts of the country where it is not available, your favorite ham will suffice.
Yield: 6 servings.

Country Sausage and Gravy

1 pound pork sausage, sliced
1 tablespoon all-purpose flour
¾ cup milk
¼ cup water
Salt and pepper to taste

In an iron skillet over medium heat brown the sausage slices on both sides. Remove to a hot platter to keep warm. Pour off all but 2 tablespoons of sausage fat from the skillet. Add the flour and stir with a wire whisk until the flour has browned. Slowly whisk in the milk and water and cook until the desired thickness. Season to taste. Pour into a warm gravy boat. Serve the sausage and gravy while they are hot.
Yield: 4 servings.

Cornmeal Mush

2 cups boiling water
2 cups milk
1 cup white cornmeal
1 teaspoon salt
½ cup cold water

In a double boiler over simmering water combine the boiling water and milk. In a small bowl combine the cornmeal, salt, and cold water. Slowly stir this mixture into the hot liquids. Cook and stir for about 5 minutes. Cover and steam for 25 to 30 minutes, stirring often. Serve as you would oatmeal with honey, molasses, or brown sugar and milk or cream.

Variation: Pour the mush into a greased loaf pan and refrigerate until chilled. Slice and fry on an oiled griddle until browned on both sides. Serve with maple syrup or molasses. This is old-time good eating!
Yield: 4 servings.

Orange Pecans

1 cup sugar
1 tablespoon light corn syrup
⅓ cup orange juice
¼ cup Jack Daniel's Whiskey
1 tablespoon butter
2½ cups pecan halves
½ teaspoon orange rind, grated

In a heavy saucepan combine the sugar, syrup, and orange juice. Cook, stirring often, until the mixture reaches the soft ball stage (240°). Remove the pan from the heat and stir in the Jack Daniel's Whiskey and butter. Beat with a wooden spoon until the mixture begins to thicken. Stir in the pecans and orange rind. Quickly drop by heaping teaspoons onto waxed paper.
Yield: 16 pieces.

Blackberry Jam

9 cups crushed blackberries (about 4 pounds)
6 cups sugar

In a large heavy saucepan combine the blackberries and sugar. Bring to a boil over medium heat, stirring frequently, until sugar dissolves. Boil for 40 minutes, stirring often, until the jam thickens. Skim off the foam with a spoon.

Quickly ladle the jam into hot sterilized jars, leaving ¼ inch headspace. Cover at once with metal lids and screw the bands tight. Process in a boiling-water bath for 15 minutes.
Yield: 3 pints.

HISTORY

In the Land of Hogs and Hominy

*This is a newspaper article dated
January 14, 1932*

With the coming of cold weather, little streams of smoke may be seen during early hours of the morning here and there at country homes as one drives along roads in this section.

Gathered around these little fires are farmers killing hogs, and women tending lard. The fine porkers swung up, ready for cutting up and salting away, bespeaks of plenty. When the smoke house is laden with meat and the corn crib is bursting with a fine crop despite the summer drought and a herd of cattle is lazily grazing in the sunken field pasture, there is no depression in the kitchen, for there is plenty to eat and plenty to spare.

Truly this section is blessed with milk and honey of honest toil. While farm prices are not what they were a year or so ago, the people are not out of employment because of closed factories as is the case in many sections. No wolf stares in at the doors here where hogs hang high and hominy is boiling in the pot and milk flows from contented cows.

Go to sections where farmers depend on a single money crop and one will see the people in the deepest blues. During the holidays this writer was in the Deep South for a few days and experienced this observation.

Truly, we are in a spot the Divine Architect fashioned with care, the beauty of country and fertility of soil would be hard to find elsewhere.

Thankful? We should be happy, for we are in a land of the blessed.

Special Pancake Syrup

2 cups good maple syrup
1 cup butter
1 teaspoon ground cinnamon
¼ teaspoon ground allspice
¼ teaspoon ground mace

In a saucepan bring all ingredients to a boil and beat with rotary beater to combine well. Serve hot syrup over pancakes or waffles for a great breakfast!
Yield: 3 cups.

Old-Fashioned Peach Preserves

2 quarts peaches, peeled and sliced
6 cups sugar

In a large glass bowl combine the peaches and sugar. Cover and store in a cool place for 12 to 18 hours. Pour the mixture into a large heavy pan and bring to a boil, stirring often. Boil gently until the peaches become transparent and the syrup thickens (about 1½ to 2 hours). Stir often to prevent the mixture from sticking or scorching. Skim off the foam with a spoon.

Quickly ladle the jam into hot sterilized jars, leaving ¼-inch headspace. Cover at once with metal lids, and screw the bands tight. Process in a boiling water bath for 15 minutes.
Yield: 7 half-pints.

Pickled Beets

2 quarts small beets
2 cups apple cider vinegar
2 cups sugar
8 whole cloves
1 stick cinnamon

In a large saucepan cook the beets in water to cover for about 15 minutes. Drain and peel.

In a small saucepan bring the vinegar, sugar, cloves, and cinnamon to a boil. Cook for 15 minutes. Meanwhile, divide the beets among hot, sterilized jars. Pour the hot vinegar over the beets, leaving ¼ inch headspace. Seal tightly.

Allow the jars to cool; store in the refrigerator, or process in boiling water bath for 30 minutes to store for later use.

Note: If larger beets are the only size available to you, then cut them into chunks or slice after peeling.
Yield: 2 quarts.

Jelly Meringue

½ cup firm jelly (or stiff preserves)
1 egg white
Pinch of salt

In a small mixing bowl combine the ingredients. With a mixer beat until the meringue is stiff and holds its own shape. This is delicious to top plain cake, shortcakes, etc., where you would use whipped cream.
Yield: 1 cup.

Miss Mary's Brother, Felix Evans

Miss Mary's brother, Felix, farmed on their mother's home place after he left school. A director at the Farmers Bank, it was mentioned in his obituary notice that all of the bank directors said they had never heard a word of criticism about Felix, who had been admired by all.

From Miss Mary's memoirs: "Felix almost died twice when he was small. The first time he was desperately ill with whooping cough. Aunt Bet Parks came and made a poultice of snuff and placed it on his chest and that saved him. Strange home remedies were used then, but they worked. The doctor had done all he knew to do to save him. Felix also almost died by drowning in the creek swollen with spring rains."

Photo courtesy of Joan Crutcher Ferguson

Real Jazzy Onions

A tangy sweet relish like those that made southern meals memorable!

¼ cup golden raisins
¼ cup Jack Daniel's Whiskey
1 pound small white onions (or pearl onions)
3 tablespoons vegetable oil
4 teaspoons brown sugar
3 large tomatoes, peeled and chopped
¼ teaspoon salt
¼ teaspoon dried thyme (or large sprig fresh thyme)
½ teaspoon freshly ground pepper

Soak the raisins in the Jack Daniel's Whiskey. Peel and clean the onions. In a large skillet heat the oil over medium heat and sauté the onions. Shake the pan until the onions are golden brown, about 5 minutes. Sprinkle the brown sugar over the onions and reduce the heat to low. Cook until the onions are caramelized, about 5 minutes. Add the tomatoes and salt and cook 5 minutes longer. Add the raisin mixture, thyme, and pepper. Transfer the mixture to a 1½-quart casserole dish. Cover. Bake in a 350° oven for 1½ hours. Remove the dish from the oven. Adjust the seasoning if desired. Cool; then refrigerate overnight. Bring to room temperature before serving.
Yield: 4 cups.

Jack Daniel's Whiskey Butter

¼ cup butter, softened
½ teaspoon dry mustard
2 teaspoons wine vinegar
2 teaspoons Worcestershire sauce
¼ teaspoon salt
Dash cayenne pepper
2 egg yolks
3 tablespoons Jack Daniel's Whiskey

In a small bowl combine all of the ingredients well. Spoon into a small crock or dish and chill until serving time.
Yield: ⅔ cup.

Spiked Cranberry Relish

When Miss Mary was alive she neither served nor cooked anything with spirits in it. However, the boarding house now serves one dish each meal made with Lynchburg's famous hometown product. The unique flavor makes these dishes special! Try this relish and see.

4 cups (1 pound) fresh cranberries
1 whole seedless orange, quartered
2 cups sugar
¼ cup Jack Daniel's Whiskey

In a food processor chop the cranberries and orange. Add the sugar and process again to combine. Place in a covered container. Chill for 24 hours. Add Jack Daniel's Whiskey just before serving. Serve this in a crystal dish, as the color is beautiful.
Yield: 1 quart.

Hot Stuff Relish

This delicious hot relish is served daily at the boarding house with peas or beans. In Moore County it is traditionally spooned onto country green beans.

2 tomatoes, chopped
1 small onion, minced
1 green pepper, minced
1 hot red pepper, seeded and finely minced
1½ tablespoons distilled white vinegar
⅓ cup water
1 tablespoon sugar
¼ teaspoon salt
⅛ teaspoon pepper

In a medium bowl combine all of the ingredients, stirring to blend well. Cover and chill. This should be made a few hours ahead of time for the best flavor.
    Note: Leftovers can be kept in the refrigerator for one or two days; any longer and the relish will get mushy.
Yield: 3 cups.

Candied Apples

6 cups apples, chopped
4 cups sugar
½ cup butter
1 tablespoon cinnamon

In a large saucepan combine all of the ingredients and cook, stirring occasionally, until the butter melts and the sugar dissolves. Pour the mixture into a greased 9 x 9-inch square baking dish. Bake at 375° for 40 minutes or until the apples are tender and the sauce is bubbly.
Yield: 8 to 10 servings.

Spiked Applesauce

¼ cup butter
3 Red Delicious apples, chopped
1 onion, chopped
⅓ cup Jack Daniel's Whiskey, warmed
2 cups chicken stock
⅓ cup heavy cream

In a large heavy skillet melt the butter. Sauté the apples and onion until tender. Pour warmed Jack Daniel's Whiskey over the apples and carefully ignite. When the flame goes out, add the chicken stock; simmer for several minutes. Add the cream and reduce heat until the sauce begins to thicken. This is delicious with pork!
Yield: 2½ cups.

Ruby Pears

1 cup cinnamon red hot candies
1 cup water
6 pears, peeled, seeded, and halved
1 3-ounce package cherry gelatin
1 3-ounce package lemon gelatin
1 cup boiling water
½ cup apple juice (or red wine)

In a skillet heat the candies in 1 cup of water until melted. Add the pears, cover and simmer for 6 minutes. Turn the pears and simmer until tender. In a heat-proof bowl dissolve the gelatins in 1 cup of boiling water; add juice (or wine). Pour the gelatin mixture over the pears, rounded side up. Broil to glaze, basting often, for about 15 minutes. Wonderful to accompany ham, pork, or poultry!
Yield: 12 servings.

Sundae Sauce

⅓ cup butter
1 cup grated coconut
½ cup firmly packed brown sugar
2 tablespoons light corn syrup
2 squares bittersweet chocolate
Dash of salt
¾ cup evaporated milk
½ teaspoon vanilla
½ pecan pieces, toasted

In a medium skillet melt the butter. Saute the coconut until golden, stirring constantly. Remove the coconut and reserve. To the butter remaining in skillet add brown sugar, corn syrup, chocolate squares, and salt. Cook and stir over very low heat until mixture bubbles vigorously. Stir in milk and bring to a boil. Boil for 1½ minutes. Remove from heat and stir in vanilla, coconut, and pecan pieces. Wonderful hot or cold over ice cream and pound cake.
Yield: 1½ cups.

Sauce for Steamed Vegetables

¼ cup butter, melted
1 cup mayonnaise
2 tablespoons horseradish
¼ teaspoon cayenne pepper
½ teaspoon Tabasco sauce
½ teaspoon salt
1 teaspoon dry mustard
2 tablespoons onion, grated

Stir all ingredients together until well mixed. Arrange steamed vegetables on a platter (cauliflower, broccoli, onions, squash, and carrots are good). Pour sauce over top of vegetables and serve. Do not heat sauce.
Yield: 1¼ cups.

Stuffed Dates

1 box pitted dates
Pecan halves
2 cans crescent rolls
Powdered sugar

Split dates open but do not cut through. Insert a pecan half into each date. Unroll crescent roll dough and cut a triangle just large enough to cover date. Pinch to seal. Brush with butter and bake at 350° until light brown, about 12 to 15 minutes. Remove from cookie sheet and roll, while hot, in powdered sugar.
Yield: 6 servings.

Soups and Salads

Summer Supper Soup

1 stewing chicken
1 large onion, peeled
1 teaspoon salt
2 carrots, sliced
1 large onion, diced
2 yellow summer squash, sliced
2 potatoes, diced
2 ribs celery, thinly sliced
2 ears of corn, cut from cob
½ small cabbage, chopped
1 cup long-grain rice, cooked
4 large fresh tomatoes, peeled and chopped (or
   one pound canned tomatoes)
1 teaspoon cumin
1 clove garlic, minced
Salt and pepper to taste
½ teaspoon dried red pepper flakes (optional)

In a large stock pot with one of the onions
and one teaspoon of salt, cook the chicken in
water to cover until done. Remove the chick-
en from the liquid, reserving the broth. Pull
the meat from the bones, discarding the skin
and bones. Strain the broth and return it to
the pan, adding enough water to equal 6 cups
of liquid. Add the remaining ingredients and
cook until vegetables are tender. Stir in the
chicken meat for the last 10 minutes of cooking. Serve hot with any type of cornbread.
Yield: 8 servings.

Moore County Mushroom Soup

¼ cup butter
½ cup onions, finely chopped
½ pound mushrooms, chopped
5 tablespoons all-purpose flour
½ teaspoon salt
⅛ teaspoon freshly ground pepper
⅛ teaspoon nutmeg
5 cups chicken broth
1 cup cream
¼ cup Jack Daniel's Whiskey
2 tablespoons parsley, chopped (optional)

In a large saucepan melt the butter. Add the
onion and sauté over medium low heat for 5
minutes, stirring often. Add the mushrooms
and cook 5 minutes more, stirring often.
Remove the pan from the heat and add the
flour, salt, pepper, and nutmeg. Stir until
smooth and well blended. Return to medium
heat. Gradually add the chicken broth, stirring constantly. Cover and simmer for 5 minutes. Stir in the cream and Jack Daniel's
Whiskey and heat through. Spoon into bowls
and garnish with chopped parsley, if desired.
Yield: 6 servings.

Old-Time Chicken and Rice Soup

½ cup long-grain rice
1¼ cups water
½ teaspoon salt
2 pounds chicken pieces (or 1 small chicken)
2 large onions, chopped
6 whole cloves
2 ribs celery, chopped
2 carrots, shredded
1½ teaspoons salt
½ teaspoon pepper
Bay leaf
½ teaspoon dried thyme
3 quarts water
Sour cream (optional)
Dill sprigs (optional)

In a small saucepan bring the rice, 1¼ cups of water, and ½ teaspoon of salt to a boil. Cover, reduce the heat to simmer, and cook until the water is absorbed, about 15 minutes.

In a large stockpot combine the remaining ingredients and bring to a boil. Reduce the heat, cover, and simmer for 45 minutes, until the chicken is tender. Skim the top as needed.

Remove the chicken and set it aside to cool. Continue to cook the liquid uncovered until reduced by ⅓. Strain and discard the vegetables and spices. Pour the strained stock back into the pot and return it to a boil. Reduce the heat. Meanwhile, pull the chicken meat from the bones, discarding the bones and skin. Cut into small chunks and return the meat to the stock. Stir in the rice. Adjust the seasonings to taste. Serve hot.

A dollop of sour cream and a dill sprig may be added to each serving to garnish, if desired.
Yield: 6 servings.

BOARDERS' STORIES

Mr. Prince

>┥╍╄╼O╾╊╍┝<

DURING THE LATE 1940s, Miss Mary kept one room in her house for the crew of a construction company. Many times there were three or four men sharing that room.

Another room was kept for the government men assigned to the Jack Daniel Distillery. Today many people refer to men who held that job as "revenuers." However, these men were well accepted by all at the boarding house and residents of Lynchburg as working members of the distillery.

Whenever people come from another part of the country their ways can seem peculiar to the local folk. Some of the government men's peculiarities earned them the reputation as characters. One such character, Mr. Prince, really enjoyed walking. However, he soon learned that if you are on foot in a small town, people who are driving will stop and insist on giving you a lift. Because Mr. Prince liked to walk, he bought a bicycle—which he never rode. He just pushed it as he walked back and forth to work. After he had had it for a while, one of the wheels fell off. Apparently this did not discourage him, as he just kept on pushing it back and forth, with only one wheel. During the winter, when it got very cold in the hollow, he took a grocery sack, cut out two holes for his eyes, put the sack over his head, picked up his bicycle, and walked to work.

Cream of Tomato Soup

2 tablespoons butter
1 large onion, minced
2 cloves garlic, minced
2 pounds ripe tomatoes, peeled and chopped
3¼ cups chicken broth (canned may be used)
2 tablespoons tomato paste
2 tablespoons cornstarch
½ teaspoon celery salt
½ teaspoon dried red pepper flakes
1 cup heavy cream
Salt
Sour cream (optional)
Fresh minced dill or sweet basil (optional)

In large saucepan melt the butter and sauté the onion and garlic until translucent. Simmer ripe tomatoes in two cups of broth. Add the remaining broth, tomatoes, tomato paste, cornstarch, celery salt, and red pepper flakes. Bring to a boil over medium high heat. Reduce the heat immediately and simmer for about 10 minutes, stirring occasionally. The soup will be thick. Carefully force the soup through a sieve. Return the soup to the pan. Stir in the cream and adjust the seasonings to taste.

Note: Excellent served with a dollop of sour cream mixed with minced fresh dill or sweet basil.
Yield: 6 servings.

Creamy Corn Soup

½ cup butter, divided
1 carrot, shredded
3 ribs celery, finely chopped
1 bell pepper, chopped
1 large onion, chopped
1 apple, chopped
⅓ cup all-purpose flour
4 cups chicken broth
¾ cup cooked chicken, cubed
2 whole cloves
4 fresh ears corn, cut from cob (scrape cob)
Salt and pepper to taste
3 cups milk (or half-and-half for richer soup)
Paprika and croutons for garnish (optional)

In a large saucepan melt ¼ cup of butter (½ stick). Add the carrot, celery, pepper, onion, and apple and sauté lightly, being careful not to brown the butter or vegetables. Push the vegetables to one side and add the remaining butter. In a small mixing bowl blend the flour with a small amount of the chicken broth. Gradually add more broth to make a smooth liquid. Pour over the vegetables and add the remaining broth, chicken cubes, and cloves. Cover and simmer for 35 minutes.

Cut the corn from the ears and then carefully scrape the ears to extract the liquid. Add the corn and the scraped liquid to the soup mixture. Season to taste. Cover and simmer for 15 additional minutes. Gently stir in the milk to blend. Bring the soup almost to the boiling point. Remove the cloves. Ladle into soup bowls and sprinkle with paprika and croutons, if desired.
Yield: 8 servings.

**Miss Mary's brother, Charlie Evans,
who later bought Uncle Hosey's mill**

*The newspaper clipping on the following page is from the
Lynchburg Falcon and was saved by Louise Crutcher. It tells an
interesting story not only about the mill, but also about the
boarding house, which is referred to in the story as "the old
Salmon House."*

Photo courtesy of Joan Crutcher Ferguson

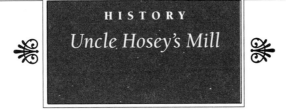

HISTORY

Uncle Hosey's Mill

This is an article from the Moore County News

UNCLE HOSEY'S MILL is now grinding out good wholesome corn meal under the management of our "Venerable Friend," Charlie Evans, who will be delighted to have you call with your "grist." Charlie will also crush your mill feed for 12½ cents per 100 pounds.

This old mill was established more than a century ago by the Dance family, when this part of the new world was still in the wilderness, at a time when there were few mills in the country. It was first equipped with two imported French burrs, one for wheat and one for corn.

The early settlers came for many miles to have their grain converted into meal and flour. They came to this mill and camped awaiting their turn. Uncle Hosey Anthony was the miller for half a century, and it became known far and wide as "Hosey's Mill," though it was always the property of the Dance family until a few years ago.

This old mill was grinding away when Andrew Jackson was fighting the southern tribes of Indians, and no doubt the meal was from this old mill that the old colored cook made the bread at the "Old Taylor Inn," one mile down the road below Lynchburg, when old Andrew Jackson lodged there on his trips through this country on his marches to war with the red skins and more than likely the bread that was served to Nathan Bedford Forrest at Uncle Felix Waggoner's that day in 1865 when the General set up quarters down the pike. Yes, and I wouldn't be afraid to bet that the meal that made the bread for Frank James at the old Salmon House when that world famous bandit visited Dr. E. Y. Salmon some time back in the seventies. And when Gov. Robert L. Taylor and many other notables of other days lodged at this old Salmon House that was famous for its good southern cooked meals.

This old Salmon House was among the first buildings erected in Lynchburg by the Roundtree family, a name that today is unknown in this section of Tennessee. But Charlie Evans' sister is the landlady of this old house, and it is still known for the good wholesome southern meals, and the meal that makes the bread today is ground at "Hosey's Old Mill."

Cabbage Soup

This is a different soup—rather sweet and sour, but rich and delicious!

1 pound stew meat
3 tablespoons bacon drippings (or oil)
Salt and pepper
1 pound head of cabbage
1 large onion, peeled and chopped
½ cup celery, chopped
1 20-ounce can stewed tomatoes
1 15-ounce can tomato sauce
¼ cup A-1 sauce
1 apple, peeled, cored, and chopped
1 cup seedless raisins
¾ cup light brown sugar
4 cups water

In a large stew pot brown the meat in bacon drippings; sprinkle with salt and pepper. Add the remaining ingredients. Bring to a boil, reduce heat, and cook for 2 hours, adding water if necessary.
   Note: One cup of cooked rice may be added to soup just long enough before serving to heat through.
Yield: 8 servings.

Corn Chowder

3 tablespoons butter
1 medium onion, chopped
4 cups fresh corn kernels (or 2 10-ounce packages frozen corn, thawed)
⅓ cup Jack Daniel's Whiskey
3 tablespoons flour
2 cups chicken stock
2 cups cream
Salt and cayenne pepper to taste
2 potatoes, cubed and cooked

In a large saucepan melt the butter over medium heat and sauté the onion for 5 minutes. Add the corn and continue to cook until the corn is slightly soft. Pour in the Jack Daniel's Whiskey and carefully ignite. Tilt the pot so the flame touches all of the corn. When the flame goes out, stir in the flour. Slowly stir in the chicken stock, cream, salt, and cayenne pepper. Heat until thickened. Add the potato cubes. Heat through; serve hot.
Yield: 8 servings.

Fish Soup

1 medium onion, peeled and chopped
2 tablespoons oil
3 cups milk
2 cups potatoes, cooked and cubed
1 16-ounce can stewed tomatoes
1 16-ounce can mixed vegetables, drained and rinsed
1 8-ounce can whole kernel corn, drained and rinsed
1 tablespoon Tabasco
1 teaspoon salt
Pepper to taste
2 pounds white fish fillets, cubed

In a large stew pot lightly saute onion in oil just until translucent. Add the milk, vegetables, and seasonings and bring to a fast simmer. Add the fish and continue to simmer for 15 minutes until fish is cooked.
   Note: Frozen vegetables can be used: substitute one 10-ounce package frozen vegetables for each can of mixed vegetables or corn.
Yield: 6 servings.

Old-Time Chicken Broth

Chicken back, wing tips, necks, and giblets
1 large onion
2 cloves garlic
2 ribs celery with leaves
2 carrots
10 peppercorns
5 whole cloves
10 whole allspice
2 bay leaves
Parsley stems
1 egg shell

In a large pot of cold water place all the ingredients. Bring to a boil, then reduce heat to a simmer. Skim off foam as it accumulates and simmer for 3 to 4 hours. Keep the pot full of water to allow for evaporation. Strain and discard bones, vegetables, etc. After the broth has been refrigerated the fat can be removed as it will harden.

   Note: The egg shell is an important ingredient. Old-fashioned cooks knew that an egg shell would keep the broth clear!
Yield: 2 quarts.

Premium Onion Soup

2 cups yellow onions, thinly sliced
3 tablespoons butter
8 cups beef broth
Pinch of powdered thyme
¼ cup Jack Daniel's Whiskey
Salt and pepper
8 pieces of French bread, toasted and thickly
   sliced
½ cup grated Parmesan cheese
½ cup grated Gruyere cheese

In a large stew pot saute the onions in butter until lightly browned. Add broth, thyme, and Jack Daniel's Whiskey. Simmer for 40 minutes. Salt and pepper to taste. Pour into individual oven-proof soup bowls. Top each with a slice of toast and a sprinkle of both cheeses. Broil until cheese is melted and lightly browned.
Yield: 8 servings.

Cheese Soup

¼ cup butter
½ cup celery, finely chopped
½ cup onions, finely chopped
½ cup carrots, finely chopped
¼ cup all-purpose flour
1 tablespoon cornstarch
4 cups milk
4 cups chicken broth
⅛ teaspoon baking soda
1 pound sharp Cheddar cheese, cubed

In a large, heavy saucepan melt the butter and sauté the vegetables until tender. Add the flour and cornstarch, stirring until smooth. Gradually add the milk and broth. Cook until thickened and bubbly. Stir in the baking soda and cheese. Reduce the heat to low and cook until the cheese melts. Serve warm.
Yield: 6 to 8 servings.

Louise's Cole Slaw

1 pound cabbage, shredded
1 medium onion, chopped
2 carrots, chopped
1 green pepper, chopped
2 teaspoons salt
½ cup white vinegar
1 tablespoon sugar
¼ cup salad oil
1 teaspoon celery seed

In a large bowl combine the vegetables. Stir to mix. Sprinkle with salt and let stand for twenty minutes. Drain any liquid that accumulates. Combine the remaining ingredients and pour over vegetables, toss to cover. Chill overnight.

Note: If you like pickles added to your cole slaw, this is a good one to add ¼ cup coarsely chopped pickles, either sweet or dill, but not both. Just combine the vegetables and toss as above.
Yield: 6 to 8 servings.

Our Favorite Slaw

1 cup vegetable oil
1 cup sugar
1 cup apple cider vinegar
2 teaspoons prepared yellow mustard
¼ cup sweet pickle relish
2 teaspoons celery seed
1 large cabbage, chopped or shredded
2 bell peppers, chopped
1 large sweet onion, chopped
Salt and pepper to taste

In a small saucepan combine the oil, sugar, vinegar, and mustard. Boil for about 5 minutes. Stir in the pickle relish and celery seed.

Remove the pan from the heat and allow the dressing to cool.

In a large salad bowl combine the cabbage, peppers, onion, and seasonings. Toss to blend. Pour the cooled dressing over the vegetables and stir to mix. Chill.

Note: Tastes best when it is made one day ahead so the flavors can meld in refrigerator.
Yield: 20 servings.

Shellie Bean and Rice Salad

1½ cups cooked rice, cooled
4 cups fresh or frozen mixed shell beans
    (speckled butter beans, black-eyed peas,
    crowder peas, purple hull beans, creme peas,
    field peas, or baby limas), cooked, drained,
    and cooled
1 cup celery, sliced
1 cup red cabbage, shredded
½ cup fresh parsley, chopped
⅓ cup green onions, sliced
⅓ cup vegetable oil
3 tablespoons apple cider vinegar
¼ teaspoon dry mustard
¼ teaspoon celery seed
Salt and pepper to taste
Hot pepper sauce to taste

In a large bowl combine the rice, beans, celery, red cabbage, parsley, and onions. In a small bowl whisk together the oil, vinegar, mustard, and celery seed. Pour the dressing over the salad mixture, tossing to blend well. Season with salt, pepper, and hot sauce. Serve chilled or at room temperature.
Yield: 8 to 10 servings.

Broccoli Salad

1 cup mayonnaise
½ cup sugar
2 tablespoons vinegar
1 head broccoli, separated into florets
½ cup raisins
¼ cup sweet red onion, chopped
½ cup pecans, toasted and chopped
½ cup sunflower seeds
½ pound bacon, cooked crisp and crumbled

In a small bowl whisk together the mayonnaise, sugar, and vinegar. In a large salad bowl combine the remaining ingredients except bacon. Add the dressing and toss well to coat. Refrigerate for several hours or overnight. Top with the bacon before serving.
Yield: 6 servings.

Best Fruit Salad

½ cup sugar
¼ teaspoon salt
¼ teaspoon paprika
3 eggs
6 tablespoons cream
2 tablespoons butter
6 tablespoons lemon juice
2 cups apple, diced
1 cup pears, diced
1 cup bananas, sliced
1 cup celery, sliced
1 cup seedless grapes, halved
1 cup pecans, toasted and chopped

In the top of a double boiler over simmering water combine the sugar, salt, and paprika. Add the eggs and cream. Cook and stir until thick. Remove the pan from the water and stir in the butter and lemon juice. Set the dressing aside to cool.

In a large salad bowl combine the fruits and nuts. When the dressing has cooled, pour it over the mixture and toss lightly.
Yield: 6 servings.

Fresh Tomato Hash

Visitors from far and near love this sweet and sour salad, served when the garden is producing lots of sweet, homegrown tomatoes.

4 medium tomatoes, chopped and drained
½ cup celery, chopped
¼ cup bell pepper, chopped
1 medium onion, thinly sliced
2 tablespoons mustard seed
1 teaspoon salt
1½ teaspoons nutmeg
½ teaspoon cinnamon
¼ teaspoon cloves
⅓ cup vinegar
3 tablespoons sugar

In a large bowl combine the tomatoes, celery, bell pepper, and onion. Set the bowl aside.

In a small bowl blend the remaining ingredients well. Pour the dressing over the vegetables and toss lightly. Cover and chill a few hours before serving.
Yield: 3 cups.

The Boarding House

From Miss Mary's memoirs: "Jack and I had always been schoolmates and neighbors. In 1902 we married in Shelbyville at a minister's home. We lived on his mother's farm for a long time, then he went into business at Estill Springs with Frank Evans, my half-brother. While we lived there Louise was born in 1905.

"We came back to Lynchburg later and moved here to the Hotel, formerly Salmon House. Charles was born in 1909 here. Mrs. Bobo, his mother, was here with us for several years. After Dr. Salmon died in 1913, we bought the property. We sure have had lots of people to stay here. Most all were fine people.

"Louise and Charles went to school here and had lots of playmates. She never could learn the piano for so much company, no practice time.

"We paid $2,500 for this home and it is in better shape now than when we bought it. It used to be called the Bobo Hotel until we took the sign down. We had a number of full-time boarders, like Tom Motlow, Will Parks, Roughton Waggoner, they all lived with us a long time. All of the rooms had two in a room. Later Mr. Tom Motlow moved downstairs to the front room. Reagor Motlow had a bath added to that room for his aging uncle.

"My life has been a happy one. I always had good help. I never had to work very hard, and that is why I had a long life."

Photo courtesy of Joan Crutcher Ferguson

Bean Salad

1 16-ounce can French-style green beans
1 16-ounce can yellow wax beans
1 16-ounce can kidney beans
1 16-ounce can whole kernel corn
½ cup onion, chopped
½ cup bell pepper, chopped
½ cup apple cider vinegar
½ cup sugar
Salt and pepper to taste

Drain and wash the canned beans and corn. In a large salad bowl combine all of the vegetables and toss lightly. In a small bowl combine the vinegar, sugar, salt, and pepper, stirring well to dissolve the sugar. Pour the dressing over the vegetables, cover, and refrigerate for several hours to allow the flavors to blend. Serve cold.
Yield: 8 to 10 servings.

Pea-Pickled Salad

Peas and beans are favored by all southerners any way that they are fixed. This is an especially good rendition of peas.

2 16-ounce cans black-eyed peas, drained and
    washed
1 large onion, thinly sliced and separated into
    rings
½ cup olive oil
¼ cup apple cider vinegar
2 cloves garlic, crushed
1 tablespoon Worcestershire sauce
1 teaspoon salt
1 bay leaf
Pepper to taste

In a heat-proof bowl combine the peas and onion. In a small saucepan combine the remaining ingredients and bring the mixture to a boil. Pour the dressing over the peas and onions. Cover and refrigerate overnight to let the flavors meld. Remove the bay leaf before serving.
Yield: 4½ cups.

Fresh Cucumber and Sour Cream Salad

2 large cucumbers
½ cup sour cream
1 tablespoon lemon juice
1 tablespoon apple cider vinegar
½ teaspoon salt
2 tablespoons chives, chopped
Lettuce leaves

Peel the cucumbers and cut them into thin slices. Place the cucumber slices in a medium bowl and set it aside.

In a small bowl combine the sour cream, lemon juice, vinegar, salt, and chives. Pour the dressing over the cucumbers and gently mix to coat. Cover the bowl and chill in the refrigerator from 2 hours to overnight. To serve, spoon the cucumbers over torn lettuce leaves.
Yield: 6 to 8 servings.

Garden Fresh Cucumber Salad

2 garden fresh cucumbers
1 tablespoon coarse salt
1 large onion, peeled and sliced
½ cup white distilled vinegar
½ cup water
Pinch of sugar

Score the cucumbers with the tines of a table fork, scraping the skin off to form ridges. Slice in ¼-inch slices and place in a bowl. Sprinkle with coarse salt. Cover and refrigerate for one hour. Remove and drain off any accumulated liquid. Add onion slices to the cucumbers. Combine water, vinegar, and sugar, and pour over the cucumbers. Cover and chill until serving time.
Yield: 6 servings.

Sweet Deviled Eggs

8 large hard-boiled eggs
½ teaspoon prepared mustard
2 tablespoons salad dressing
3 tablespoons sweet pickle relish
Paprika
Fresh parsley, sliced stuffed olives, or dill sprigs
   as garnish (optional)

Slice the eggs in half lengthwise and carefully remove the yolks. In a medium bowl mash the yolks and add the mustard, salad dressing, and pickle relish, stirring until smooth. Spoon or pipe into the egg whites. Sprinkle with paprika and garnish, if desired.
Yield: 16 servings.

Refreshing Lime Salad

2 3-ounce packages lime gelatin
2 cups boiling water
1 cup mayonnaise
1 cup creamy cottage cheese
1 cup crushed pineapple with juice
½ cup pimiento-stuffed olives, drained and
   chopped

In an 8-inch square Pyrex dish dissolve the gelatin in the boiling water. Cover and chill until cool. In a separate bowl mix the remaining ingredients and stir into the cooled gelatin. Refrigerate until congealed. To serve, cut into squares and serve on lettuce leaves.
Yield: 10 to 12 servings.

Tuna in Aspic

3 cups V-8 juice
1 6-ounce package lemon gelatin
½ cup vinegar
1 16-ounce can tuna, well drained
1 10-ounce package mixed vegetables, cooked
and well drained
1 medium onion, peeled and coarsely chopped
1 medium pepper, cored, seeded, and chopped
½ cup celery, chopped
Salt and pepper

In a small saucepan heat juice to boiling. Remove from heat and dissolve gelatin in hot liquid. Chill until slightly thickened. Add remaining ingredients. Pour into a square 2-quart serving dish, cover, and refrigerate. To serve, cut into squares and serve on lettuce leaf with dollop of mayonnaise and a boiled egg half, if desired.
Yield: 8 to 10 servings.

Simple Supper Tomatoes

Traditionally, this was prepared after mid-day dinner with any leftover tomato slices, adding enough for the supper table.

6 large, firm, ripe tomatoes, sliced
1 bunch green onions, sliced, including half of
   green tops
2 tablespoons parsley, minced
2 tablespoons sweet basil, minced (optional)
Salt and pepper to taste
¾ cup olive oil (or salad oil)
¼ cup apple cider vinegar
1 clove garlic, pressed to release juice
1 teaspoon sugar
1 teaspoon salt
1 teaspoon Worcestershire sauce

In a large glass salad bowl layer the tomatoes and onions. Sprinkle with parsley, basil, salt, and pepper. In a small mixing bowl blend the oil, vinegar, garlic, sugar, salt, and Worcestershire sauce with a wire whisk or electric mixer to combine and blend well. Spoon over the tomato slices. Cover the dish and chill until suppertime.
Yield: 6 servings.

Pork Loaf

2 pounds pork tenderloin
1 large onion
2 hard-boiled eggs
2 sprigs fresh dill
1 rib celery, chopped
2 carrots, shredded
1 package unflavored gelatin
½ cup cold water
Salt and freshly ground pepper to taste
Tomatoes, cucumbers, and dill pickles for
   garnish

In a large stock pot cover the meat with water and cook slowly until tender. Drain the broth, reserving 2 cups for the gelatin. Slice half of the onion and both eggs. Arrange the onion rings, egg slices, and sprigs of dill in the bottom of a 1½-quart mold. Chop the remaining part of the onion. Combine with the celery and carrots and set aside.

In a medium saucepan sprinkle the gelatin over the cold water, stirring to dissolve. Add the reserved broth and bring the mixture to a boil. In a food processor chop the meat and stir it into the hot broth with the carrots, onion, celery, and seasonings. Carefully spoon into the mold, cover with foil, and place in the refrigerator to chill until set. Serve with sliced fresh tomatoes, cucumbers, and crisp dill pickles as a garnish.
Yield: 8 servings.

Thousand Island Dressing

1 cup mayonnaise
4 tablespoons thick catsup
1 teaspoon Worcestershire sauce
6 tablespoons chili sauce
¼ cup sweet pickle relish
Salt and pepper to taste

Mix all the ingredients to blend well. Cover and refrigerate until ready to use. Excellent to top Pork Loaf.
Yield: 1½ cups.

Hot Bacon Dressing

10 slices bacon
¾ cup apple cider vinegar
¾ cup all-purpose flour
1¼ cups water
¾ cup sugar
¼ teaspoon salt
1 cup water

In a large skillet fry the bacon until crisp, reserving the drippings. Remove the slices and crumble into small bits. Meanwhile, add the vinegar to the bacon drippings in the skillet and bring to a boil. Make a paste with the flour and water, stir until smooth, and add to boiling vinegar. Add the sugar, salt, and remaining water, along with the bacon bits. Continue to boil for approximately 5 minutes. Serve the hot dressing over hot potatoes and chopped onions to produce a German-type potato salad, or serve warm dressing over tossed salad or spinach leaves with grapefruit or orange sections and rings of sweet red onion.
Yield: 1½ cups.

Virgin Vinaigrette

1 clove garlic, minced
¾ teaspoon salt
½ cup tomato juice (or V-8 juice)
3 tablespoons red wine vinegar
1 teaspoon Worcestershire sauce
1 teaspoon tomato paste
½ teaspoon freshly ground pepper
¼ cup celery leaves, minced
*2 dashes hot pepper sauce (Tennessee Sunshine
   is good)*
½ cup olive oil

In a medium mixing bowl whisk together all of the ingredients except the oil. Slowly whisk in the oil. This is a zesty dressing for salads. The dressing will keep for three days in the refrigerator.
Yield: 1¼ cups.

Hot Potato Salad

12 large potatoes
6 slices bacon
Salad oil
10 green onions, chopped
½ cup sugar
Salt to taste
½ teaspoon freshly ground pepper
½ teaspoon dry mustard
1 cup chicken broth

In a large pan boil the potatoes in enough water to cover. While the potatoes are cooking, fry the bacon until crisp. Remove the bacon and drain on a paper towel. Pour the bacon drippings into a heat-resistant measuring cup. Add enough to salad oil to measure ½ cup. Set aside.

When the potatoes are just tender, drain the liquid, peel, and dice. Place in a large salad bowl with the crumbled bacon and onions. Cover to keep hot.

Using the same skillet, combine the bacon drippings with the remaining ingredients. Bring to a boil. Remove the pan from the heat and pour over the potato mixture. Stir to blend. Serve hot (or cold if you have any leftovers).
Yield: 12 servings.

Pecan Chicken Salad

8 cups cooked chicken, diced
Salt to taste
2 cups celery, diced
1½ cups bell pepper, chopped
1½ cups pecans, chopped
1 cup apple, chopped
1 cup raisins, softened (soak in boiling water to
   soften, drain)
2 cups mayonnaise
2 10½-ounce cans cream of chicken soup
4 hard-boiled eggs, chopped
1½ cups potato chips, crushed
1 cup Cheddar cheese, grated

In a large bowl mix the chicken, salt, celery, bell pepper, pecans, apple, raisins, mayonnaise, soup, and eggs. Stir to blend. Pour into a large casserole dish. Layer with the potato chip crumbs, then top with cheese. Bake at 350° for 25 minutes.
Yield: 20 servings.

Mama's Slaw

1 small cabbage, shredded
2 carrots, grated
1 onion, chopped
2 tablespoons sugar
1½ cups salad dressing
½ cup vinegar
Salt and pepper to taste

In a large salad bowl toss the prepared vegetables to mix well. Add the remaining ingredients and mix very well. Cover and chill for at least 3 hours.
Yield: 12 servings.

Macaroni Salad

1 16-ounce package elbow macaroni
½ cup green pepper, finely chopped
½ cup onion, minced
½ cup stewed tomatoes, well drained
1 cup salad dressing (such as Miracle Whip)
Salt and pepper

In a large saucepan cook the macaroni according to the package directions and drain. In a large bowl combine the remaining ingredients. Add the cooked macaroni and stir to blend. Cover and refrigerate for at least 2 hours before serving. Add more salad dressing if it becomes too dry.
Yield: 8 servings.

Salmon Salad

1 15½-ounce can red sockeye salmon
1 cup mashed potatoes, seasoned with butter,
   salt, and pepper
4 tablespoons sweet pickle relish
1 onion, chopped
2 hard-boiled eggs, chopped
½ cup salad dressing (or mayonnaise)

Drain the salmon, remove the skin, and flake. Add the potatoes, pickle relish, onion, and eggs. Mix gently with the salad dressing to blend. Chill until serving time. May be served on lettuce leaves, as a sandwich spread, or on crackers for an appetizer.
Yield: 6 to 8 servings.

Picnic Potato Salad

8 large potatoes
4 hard-boiled eggs, divided
1 cup salad dressing
1 4-ounce jar pimientos, chopped
1 cup celery, finely chopped
1 cup Cheddar cheese, shredded
1 cup sweet pickles, chopped
1 cup stuffed olives, chopped
Salt and pepper to taste
Garnish of choice: paprika, fresh dill, or
* parsley*

In a large saucepan boil the unpeeled pota-toes in water to cover until they are tender and can easily be pierced with a fork. Drain and cool. Remove skins and dice potatoes. Peel and chop 3 of the eggs. In a large bowl combine the potatoes and eggs. Stir in all of the remaining ingredients and turn with a spoon until well blended. Adjust the season-ings to taste. (A little sweet pickle juice may be added to moisten and brighten the flavor.) Spoon into a glass salad bowl and chill until serving time. Garnish with paprika, a fresh dill sprig, or parsley and reserved egg, sliced. *Yield: 12 servings.*

Easy Fruit Salad

Combine any amount of fresh, frozen, or drained canned fruits. Choose your favorites: bananas, pineapple, apples, orange segments, cherries, strawberries, cantaloupe, honeydew or grapes. Use canned peach pie filling as a dressing. Cover and chill thoroughly before serving . . . *yummy!*

Party Salad

This fruit salad is a hit at all dinner parties!

2 tablespoons butter
2 tablespoons sugar
2 eggs, beaten
2 tablespoons lemon juice
2 cups seedless grapes (use half green and half
* red for color)*
1 16-ounce can pineapple tidbits, drained
2 8-ounce cans Mandarin oranges, drained
1 16-ounce can fruit cocktail, drained
2 cups miniature marshmallows
1 cup whipping cream
2 tablespoons sugar

In a small saucepan over medium heat, cook the butter, 2 tablespoons sugar, eggs, and lemon juice, stirring constantly until thick. Set aside the dressing to cool.

In a large bowl combine the fruits and marshmallows. Pour the cooled dressing over mixture and toss to mix well. In a sepa-rate bowl whip the cream, gradually adding the sugar. Carefully fold the whipped cream into fruit. Chill for 8 hours before serving. *Yield: 10 to 12 servings.*

Christmas Dinner at the Boarding House

Christmas dinner at the boarding house and Miss Mary is serving her famous baked hen and dressing to her daughter, Louise Crutcher, and husband Ervin (at the other end of the table). Clarence and Elvie Rolman are at the center of the table and Herb and Nell Fanning are in the foreground. Herb Fanning, the Rolmans, and Miss Mary are well known to those who have followed the Jack Daniel's ads. Also, Clarence and Herb are well known for their humorous retorts. When television personality Spencer Christian in an interview asked Herb how old he was, he replied, "Oh, I'm so old I don't buy green bananas anymore." Clarence said on his 90th birthday, "I'm living and glad of it. You wouldn't believe it, but people are dying to get in the graveyard today."

Old-Time Fruit Dressing

2 eggs, beaten
2 tablespoons sugar
2 tablespoons lemon juice (or vinegar can be
   used)
2 tablespoons pineapple juice
1 tablespoon butter
Dash of salt
¼ cup whipping cream, chilled

In a small saucepan, combine the eggs, sugar, juices, butter, and salt. Heat just to boiling, stirring constantly. Remove from heat and let cool. In a chilled bowl beat the whipping cream until stiff. Fold the cream into egg mixture. Pour over a salad of drained canned fruits: cherries, pineapple, orange segments, and marshmallows. Allow the flavors to meld overnight in the refrigerator. Delicious!

Note: Pineapple juice can be taken from pineapple syrup off of pineapple used in salad.

Yield: 1¼ cups.

Sweet Pepper Salad

2 large green peppers
2 large red peppers
2 large tomatoes
2 medium sweet onions
3 tablespoons salad oil
3 tablespoons cider vinegar
1 teaspoon Dijon mustard
1 teaspoon sweet basil (fresh or dried)
Salt and pepper

Core and seed the peppers, slicing into thin strips. Peel and slice the tomatoes and onions. In a bowl layer the pepper strips, tomato slices, and onion rings. Set aside.

In a bowl or cruet stir or shake the remaining ingredients to blend. Pour over the vegetables. Cover and refrigerate until well chilled, about two hours. This is excellent made the day before so the vegetables really have time to marinate. To serve, toss to blend and garnish with chopped parsley and grated cheese, if desired.

Yield: 8 servings.

Breads

Breakfast Popovers

2 eggs
1 cup milk
2 tablespoons butter, melted
1 cup all-purpose flour
½ teaspoon salt
½ teaspoon nutmeg
6 teaspoons oil (or bacon drippings)

In a medium mixing bowl beat the eggs with an electric mixer at high speed. Lower the speed and add the milk and butter. Add the flour, salt, and nutmeg and blend just until smooth. It is important not to overbeat popover batter.

Place 1 teaspoon of oil in each muffin cup (or popover cups, if available); tilt to spread oil up sides of cups. Fill each cup half full with batter. Bake at 425° for 30 to 35 minutes. Popovers should be well browned and firm. With a sharp paring knife, pierce the tops of the popovers to allow the steam to escape. Return to the oven for an additional 5 minutes. Loosen the edges with a knife and serve immediately.

Excellent with homemade strawberry preserves!
Yield: 6 popovers.

Pumpkin Bread

4 eggs
2 cups sugar
1½ cups vegetable oil
1 16-ounce can pumpkin
3 cups all-purpose flour
2 teaspoons baking powder
2 teaspoons baking soda
1 teaspoon salt
2 teaspoons cinnamon
½ teaspoon nutmeg
¼ teaspoon ground cloves
1 cup seedless raisins
½ cup walnuts, chopped

Grease and flour 2 9 x 5 x 3-inch loaf pans. In a large mixing bowl beat the eggs with an electric mixer until light and golden. Add the sugar, oil, and pumpkin, blending well. In a separate bowl combine the dry ingredients. Mix well with the pumpkin mixture. Stir in the raisins and walnuts. Pour the batter into the prepared pans. Bake at 350° for 1 hour, or until a cake tester inserted in the center comes out clean. Cool upside down on a wire rack for 10 minutes before removing from the pans. Wrap in foil to store.

Delicious spread with cream cheese and served with a chicken- or fruit-salad plate.
Yield: 2 loaves.

Lynchburg Lemonade Tea Loaf

1½ cups all-purpose flour
1 teaspoon salt
1 teaspoon baking powder
Rind of 1 lemon, grated
6 tablespoons shortening
1 cup sugar
2 eggs, well beaten
½ cup milk
½ cup pecans, chopped

Grease an 8 x 4 x 3-inch loaf pan. In a small bowl combine the flour, salt, baking powder, and grated rind. Set the bowl aside.

In a large mixing bowl cream shortening and sugar until light and fluffy. Add the eggs and continue beating. Add the dry ingredients and then the milk; beat just until smooth. Stir in the chopped pecans. Pour the batter into the prepared loaf pan. Bake at 350° for 45 to 50 minutes, or until a cake tester inserted in the center comes out clean. Cool the pan on a wire rack. Prepare the sauce:

Sauce

Juice of 1 lemon
1 cup sugar
¼ cup Jack Daniel's Whiskey

Combine the ingredients and stir until sugar is dissolved. Poke holes in the tea loaf. Spoon the sauce over the top of the hot loaf, allowing the sauce to penetrate and seep down the sides of the loaf pan. Do not remove from the pan until the sauce has pen-etrated the loaf and been absorbed. Remove to a wire rack and cool.

Excellent as it is, or slices may be spread lightly with cream cheese for finger sandwiches and served with a fruit-salad plate for a bride's luncheon.
Yield: 1 loaf.

Eady's Old-Fashioned 'Lasses Rolls

1 cup oats (quick-cooking or old-fashioned)
1½ cups boiling water
½ cup molasses
⅓ cup shortening
1 teaspoon salt
2 packages active dry yeast
½ cup warm water (110°)
2 eggs, slightly beaten
6 to 6½ cups all-purpose flour

Place the oats in a large mixing bowl and pour the boiling water over them. Add the molasses, shortening, and salt and stir to blend. Set aside to cool.

In a small bowl dissolve the yeast in warm water (1 teaspoon of sugar may be added to activate the yeast quickly). Set the bowl aside.

When the oat mixture is lukewarm add the yeast, eggs, and half of the flour and beat until smooth. Stir in the remaining flour 1 cup at a time to make a soft dough. Turn the dough out onto a floured board and knead until smooth and elastic, about 5 minutes. Grease a bowl and turn the ball of dough over in the bowl to grease the top. Cover and let the dough rise in a warm, draft-free place for about 1 hour, until double in bulk.

Punch the dough down and shape into golf-ball-size balls. Place on a greased baking sheet. Cover with a light towel and let the dough rise again for about 30 to 40 minutes. (For a crusty outside, just before baking brush the rolls with 1 egg white beaten with 1 teaspoon of water.) Bake at 350° for 15 to 20 minutes.

Remove the rolls from the oven and brush the tops with melted butter, if desired. Serve immediately.

Yield: 3 dozen rolls.

HISTORY
Lynchburg's Safes

MR. TOM MOTLOW, president of the Farmers Bank in Lynchburg and long-time resident of the boarding house, told a story about the bank's six-ton safe. After the charter for the new bank was awarded on April 25, 1888, a safe was purchased. People had been traveling from Shelbyville, Fayetteville, and Lynchburg to Tullahoma for their banking services. Jack Daniel was one of the original incorporators. A building was purchased from John Eaton on the north side of the square and a safe was ordered, which was shipped via railroad to Tullahoma. The problem was how to get the safe to Lynchburg, over rough, unpaved country roads. The old Chattanooga Pike was ruled out for travel because the bridges on the road weren't strong enough to support the weight of the safe, the wagon, and the mules.

The safe was loaded on the stoutest wagon that could be found in Tullahoma, and four very strong mules were picked to pull it. The mules would have to ford several streams that crisscrossed the countryside. Finally, after the constant heavy pulling, the over-strained wagon got mired down above its axles. Jack Daniel hastily dispatched additional horses and good pulling mules to the mired wagon. The wagon didn't budge an inch. Sending an urgent message to Mr. Green, who hauled logs to his distillery, he asked that he bring his logging wagon and team of eight to get the safe moving again. They had to physically move the safe from one wagon to the other so that they could transport it on to Lynchburg.

It took more than a month to move the safe from Tullahoma to Lynchburg, a distance of fifteen miles. However, this worked to an advantage for the new bank. People felt that the bank was perfectly safe for their deposits. Anyone wishing to make off with the safe and their deposits would certainly be apprehended before they got very far.

Fresh Zucchini Bread

3 eggs
1 cup oil
1½ cups sugar
3 cups all-purpose flour
1 teaspoon baking powder
1 teaspoon salt
1 teaspoon cinnamon
¼ teaspoon baking soda
2 cups fresh zucchini, shredded

Grease and flour 2 9 x 5 x 3-inch loaf pans. In a large mixing bowl beat the eggs until light and golden. Add the oil and sugar, and blend well. In a separate bowl combine the dry ingredients. Stir in the shredded zucchini to coat. Add the dry ingredients to the egg mixture and stir to blend. Pour the batter into the prepared pans. Bake at 350° for 55 to 60 minutes or until a cake tester inserted in the center comes out clean. Place the pan upside down on a wire rack to cool for 5 to 10 minutes. Remove the bread from the pan and allow it to finish cooling. Wrap in foil to store.

This is an excellent accompaniment to fruit or chicken salad.
Yield: 2 loaves.

Boarding House Pocket-Book Rolls

These are favorites of all the boarding house guests!

2 packages active dry yeast
¼ cup lukewarm water (110°)
5 cups self-rising flour
½ teaspoon baking soda
6 tablespoons sugar
1 cup shortening or lard
2 cups buttermilk
Melted butter

In a small bowl dissolve the yeast in the lukewarm water. Set the bowl aside.

In a separate bowl combine the flour, baking soda, and sugar. Cut in the shortening. Add the yeast mixture, then add the buttermilk. Mix the batter by hand until a dough is formed. Cover the dough and place it in the refrigerator overnight.

Two hours before serving, remove the dough from the refrigerator and place it on a floured board. Punch down (dough will rise some, even in the refrigerator) and knead slightly. Roll the dough out to ½-inch thickness. Cut out with a biscuit cutter. Brush the tops with melted butter and fold over. Place on a well-greased baking sheet. Cover and place in a warm, draft-free place to rise, about 1 hour.

Rebrush the tops of the rolls with melted butter. Bake at 375° for 15 minutes, or until golden brown. Serve immediately.

Note: For home use, dough can be kept in refrigerator for as long as two weeks.
Yield: 3 to 4 dozen rolls.

Our Favorite Raisin Bread

This is wonderful toasted for breakfast!

1 cup raisins
1 teaspoon baking soda
½ cup boiling water
½ cup Jack Daniel's Whiskey
1½ cups all-purpose flour
½ cup sugar
½ teaspoon salt
1 egg, slightly beaten
1 tablespoon salad oil

Grease and flour a 9 x 5 x 3-inch loaf pan. In a small bowl combine the raisins, baking soda, boiling water, and Jack Daniel's Whiskey. Set the bowl aside.

In a medium mixing bowl combine the flour, sugar, and salt. Add the raisin mixture, egg, and oil and stir to blend. Pour the batter into the prepared pan. Bake at 350° for 35 to 45 minutes.

Note: If taking to a friend as a gift, you may ice the cooled loaf with a simple confectioners' sugar icing, wrap in plastic wrap, and tie with yarn.
Yield: 1 loaf.

Traditional Cornbread

2 tablespoons cooking oil or lard
2 cups white cornmeal
1 teaspoon baking soda
½ teaspoon salt
2 eggs, slightly beaten
1 cup buttermilk

In a 9-inch cast-iron skillet heat the oil while the oven preheats and the batter is being prepared. In a medium mixing bowl combine the cornmeal, baking soda, and salt. Add the eggs, then the buttermilk, and stir until just moistened. The batter should not be overmixed.

Remove the skillet from the oven and tilt slightly to make sure the oil has greased the bottom of the skillet, then pour the hot oil into the batter. Stir to blend. Pour the batter into the hot skillet. Bake at 350° for 20 to 25 minutes or until a cake tester inserted in the center comes out clean.

Note: The iron skillet was and is an essential utensil in Miss Mary's kitchen, just as it has been in kitchens of all good southern cooks. Using a skillet for cooking cornbread gives a crisp outer edge and browns the bread beautifully.
Yield: 8 servings.

Hot Water Hoe Cakes

1½ cups white cornmeal
1 teaspoon sugar
½ teaspoon salt
2¼ cups boiling water
Vegetable oil for oiling griddle

In a medium Pyrex bowl combine the cornmeal, sugar, and salt. Stir in the boiling water. Heat a griddle or large skillet and oil it lightly. Drop the batter by one large spoonful per hoe cake onto the griddle. Cook until browned on one side. Turn and brown the other side. Serve immediately with plenty of butter.
Yield: 4 servings.

Corn Light Bread

This is traditionally served with barbecued pork everywhere in the South.

¼ cup butter
2 cups white cornmeal
1 cup all-purpose flour
½ teaspoon salt
¼ cup sugar
1 teaspoon baking powder
½ teaspoon baking soda
1 package active dry yeast
2½ cups buttermilk, heated to lukewarm

In a cast-iron skillet over low heat melt the butter, tilting and rotating the skillet to allow the butter to coat the sides. Set the skillet aside.

In a medium mixing bowl stir together the cornmeal, flour, salt, sugar, baking powder, baking soda, and yeast. Add the buttermilk and stir to blend. Pour the batter into the prepared skillet. Cover the skillet and set it aside in a warm, draft-free place for batter to rise, about 30 minutes.

Bake at 350° for 30 minutes, or until a cake tester inserted in center comes out clean. This bread is good hot or cold. This may also be baked in loaf pans, but you should use dark-colored pans to assure a crispier outside.
Yield: 10 servings.

Angel Biscuits

1 cup buttermilk
1 package active dry yeast
1 teaspoon sugar
2½ cups all-purpose flour
1 teaspoon baking soda
1 teaspoon salt
½ cup shortening or lard
¼ cup butter, chilled
Flour
2 tablespoons butter, melted

In a small saucepan heat the buttermilk to lukewarm. Remove the pan from the heat and stir in the yeast and sugar. In a large mixing bowl stir together the flour, baking soda, and salt. Cut the shortening and ¼ cup butter into the flour mixture with a pastry blender or two knives until it resembles coarse cornmeal. Stir in the buttermilk and dry yeast until blended.

Turn the dough out onto a floured bread board and roll to ½-inch thickness. Brush the top with the melted butter. Cut into rounds with a biscuit cutter and place buttered side down on a well-greased baking sheet, close together but not touching. Brush the tops with the remaining melted butter. Cover with a sheet of plastic wrap and set aside to rise in a warm, draft-free spot for 60 minutes. Bake at 425° for about 20 minutes or until the tops are golden brown. Serve immediately.
Yield: 20 biscuits.

Family, Boarders, and Staff, Circa 1920

This photo was taken around 1920, on the porch of the boarding house. Jack Bobo is on the left with his son, Charles, in front of him. Miss Mary is just behind her daughter, Louise, and her mother, Bird, is seated in front of them with a dark flowered dress. Mrs. Callie Bobo, Jack's mother, is the first lady seated on the left. The little girl next to the post is Miss Mary's niece, Mary Avon Motlow,

daughter of Ophelia, who is standing second from the right. The cooks here are Louella Newsom and Nathaniel Ingle. Will Parks is the other man on the back row. He owned a number of businesses in Lynchburg, notably the Ford dealership. He lived at the boarding house until his death in his nineties, occupying the first room downstairs on the left. After Will's death, Mr. Tom took that room.

Hush Puppies

2 cups white cornmeal
¼ cup all-purpose flour
1 teaspoon baking powder
½ teaspoon baking soda
½ teaspoon salt
½ teaspoon pepper
2 tablespoons brown sugar
½ cup onion, finely chopped
¼ cup green pepper, finely chopped
½ cup buttermilk
⅔ cup water
½ cup bacon drippings (or butter)
1 egg, beaten
Vegetable oil for frying

In a large mixing bowl combine the dry ingredients, onion, and green pepper. In a separate bowl combine the buttermilk, water, bacon drippings, and egg. Stir the liquids into the cornmeal mixture. Drop by the spoonful into hot oil (375°). Fry until golden brown. Drain on paper towels and serve hot.
Yield: 2½ dozen.

Baking Powder Biscuits

2 cups all-purpose flour, sifted
3 teaspoons baking powder
½ teaspoon salt
6 tablespoons butter (or shortening, or a combination of both)
¾ cup milk

In a medium mixing bowl sift the flour with the baking powder and salt. Cut in the butter until the mixture resembles coarse cornmeal. Stir the milk into the mixture until the dough forms a ball. Turn the dough onto a lightly floured surface and knead several times. Roll with a floured rolling pin to ½-inch thickness. Cut with a 2-inch biscuit cutter and place on an ungreased cookie sheet. Bake at 450° for 10 to 15 minutes, or until golden brown.
Yield: 12 biscuits.

Cornmeal Biscuits

1½ cups all-purpose flour, sifted
¾ cup cornmeal
¼ teaspoon baking soda
3 teaspoons baking powder
1 teaspoon salt
1 tablespoon sugar
4 tablespoons butter
1 egg, beaten
½ cup buttermilk or sour milk
Butter

In a medium mixing bowl sift the dry ingredients together. Cut in the butter. In a small bowl mix the egg with the buttermilk. Add the liquids to the dry ingredients and stir until the dough forms a ball. Turn onto a floured board and knead slightly. Roll out to ½-inch thickness and cut with a biscuit cutter. Brush with butter and fold over into a half-moon shape. Bake at 450° for 12 to 15 minutes, or until golden brown.
Yield: 24 biscuits.

Country Loaf Bread

2 packages active dry yeast
2 cups warm water (110°)
½ cup sugar, divided
2 eggs, beaten
¼ cup vegetable oil
1 teaspoon salt
6 cups all-purpose flour

In a small bowl dissolve the yeast in warm water. Add 1 tablespoon of sugar and stir. Set aside for 5 minutes.

In a large bowl whisk together the remaining sugar, eggs, oil, and salt. Add the yeast mixture and half of the flour, mixing well. Gradually stir in the remaining flour. Turn the dough out onto a lightly floured surface. Knead for 8 to 10 minutes, or until smooth and elastic. Shape the dough into a ball. Place in a well-greased bowl, turning once to grease the top. Cover and set aside to rise in a warm draft-free area until double in size, about 1½ to 2 hours. (Hint: When dough is properly risen, an imprint will remain when you press lightly with your fingers.)

Grease 2 9 x 5 x 3-inch loaf pans. Punch the dough down and divide it in half. Place the dough on a floured surface. Roll each half into a rectangular shape. Beginning at the narrow edge, roll up the dough, pressing firmly to eliminate air pockets. Place the loaves seam-side down into the prepared pans. Brush the tops lightly with oil. Cover the loaves and set them aside to rise again until almost double in size.

Bake at 350° on the lower rack of the oven for 30 to 35 minutes, or until the loaves sound hollow when tapped on the bottom. Remove at once from the pans. Cool on a wire rack before serving.
Yield: 2 loaves.

Fresh Corn Cakes

2½ cups fresh corn kernels (see below)
2 eggs
2 tablespoons all-purpose flour
½ teaspoon salt
1 tablespoon sugar
Bacon drippings

Husk, silk, and wash fresh ears of corn. With a sharp knife, cut into the kernels by paring down through the top, then cut again close to the cob. After the kernels are off the cob, scrape the cob with the flat side of knife to remove all kernels and milk.

In a medium mixing bowl beat the eggs. Add the dry ingredients and blend. Stir in the fresh corn.

Heat a skillet or griddle with a small amount of bacon drippings to oil the surface. Drop the batter by spoonfuls onto the hot skillet. Fry until the edges are crisp, then turn and brown on the other side. Serve with butter as follows.

Corn Cakes Butter

1 teaspoon bottled hot sauce (Tennessee
*   Sunshine is good)*
½ cup butter, softened

Add hot sauce to softened butter and stir to blend. Spread on hot corn cakes. These corn cakes are excellent with country ham.
Yield: 4 to 6 servings.

Fried Grits

2 cups cooked grits
1 egg, slightly beaten
1 tablespoon water
½ cup cornflakes (or bread crumbs), finely
   crushed
¼ cup bacon drippings (or vegetable oil)

Cook the grits according to the directions on the package to yield 2 cups of cooked grits. Pour into a pan so that it will be about ½ inch deep. Refrigerate overnight. Cut the chilled grits in squares. In a shallow dish combine the beaten egg and water. Dip the squares into the beaten egg mixture and then roll them in the crumbs. Heat the bacon drippings in a heavy skillet (iron works great) and slowly brown the squares on all sides.

These squares are served for breakfast with homemade preserves or syrup.
Yield: 6 servings.

Butter Cream Muffins

½ cup butter
1½ cups sugar
½ teaspoon salt
4 eggs, well beaten
1 teaspoon baking soda
Dash nutmeg
2¾ cups all-purpose flour
1½ cups sour cream
½ cup broken pecan pieces
3 tablespoons butter, melted
¾ cup dark brown sugar
¼ cup Jack Daniel's Whiskey

In a medium mixing bowl cream together the butter, sugar, and salt, and beat until fluffy. Add the eggs, baking soda, and nutmeg. Add the flour and sour cream alternately, stirring just to blend. Set the batter aside.

Place the pecan pieces on the bottom of 12 well-greased muffin cups. In a small bowl blend the butter, brown sugar, and Jack Daniel's Whiskey. Place a spoonful of this mixture over the pecan pieces. Then fill each muffin cup ⅔ full with batter. Bake at 450° for 15 minutes. Serve at once.
Yield: 12 muffins.

Never-Fail Sweet Potato Rolls

1 package active dry yeast
1½ cups warm water (110°)
¼ cup sugar, divided
1 teaspoon salt
7 cups all-purpose flour
⅔ cup shortening
1 cup mashed sweet potatoes, slightly warm
2 eggs, slightly beaten
Butter, softened
1 egg white
2 teaspoons water

In a small bowl sprinkle the yeast over the water and add 2 tablespoons of the sugar. Stir to blend and start the yeast to dissolve. In a large mixing bowl combine the remaining sugar, salt, and 4 cups of the flour. Blend in the shortening with your fingertips. Add the yeast, sweet potatoes, eggs, and remaining flour. Turn the dough onto a floured board and knead until smooth and elastic. Place the dough in a greased bowl, turning to grease the top of dough. Cover with foil or plastic film and refrigerate.

Two hours prior to baking, remove the dough from the refrigerator and divide into 2 balls. On a floured board roll the dough out to a large circle, about ¼ inch thick. Gently spread with soft butter. Cut into 16 pie-shaped wedges. Roll up each piece, begin-

ning with the larger end. Tuck the points under and place on a baking sheet. Let the rolls rise for 1 hour. In a small cup beat the egg white with a fork until thick and foamy. Add water to blend. With a pastry brush, gently brush the tops of the rolls. Bake at 400° for 15 to 20 minutes.

Serve hot with butter....*umm, good!*
Yield: 32 rolls.

HISTORY
Miss Mary's Grandchildren

JOAN FERGUSON, daughter of Louise and Ervin Crutcher, lived next door to her grandparents, Mary and Jack Bobo, while she was growing up. She has many wonderful memories of them and of her happy childhood. As children she and her older brothers, Cliffe and Jack, had the run of the boarding house, sliding down the staircase banister, playing with dolls on the balcony over the front door, and playing kick the can in the side yard. Cops and robbers were a favorite game, with the springhouse serving as the jail because the slatted door reminded the children of a cell.

Joan's family ate its mid-day meal at the boarding house every day, and the boarders enjoyed the children being there. Roughton Waggoner was a boarder at the house for as long as Joan can remember. He owned a store on the square, where the gazebo park stands today. Once Roughton went to the World's Fair and brought Joan a china dog as a souvenir. He also paid for her tap dance lessons

with Mary B. Parks. Mr. Waggoner lived at the boarding house until he died.

In the summertime, Sunday dinner after church included homemade ice cream. After it was frozen, it was packed down and placed in the spring under the house. Miss Mary always made delicious chocolate syrup to pour over the ice cream. The spring was always kept clean and had plenty of clear water in it. On summer days there would be watermelons cooling there until serving time.

Joan and her brothers called their grandparents Mama and Papa. Jack always wore a suit, white shirt, tie, and a dress hat. He really enjoyed politics and working the crossword puzzles in the paper. He had a variety of business endeavors over the years, including owning an ice house. When unexpected crowds came to the hotel he would get very nervous and pace back and forth, while Miss Mary stayed calm in all situations.

Welcome to Lynchburg (pop. 361), Tennessee

Lynchburg (pop. 361), Tennessee, the tiny town that Jack Daniel made famous. In the background is the Visitors Welcome sign, which greets more than 250,000 visitors annually to a free tour of the distillery. It is these visitors that vye for a seat at the boarding house for a scrumptious mid-day dinner. It is best to eat first and tour after dinner. Then you have a chance to walk off that extra helping of everything that you couldn't resist at the table.

Cracklin' Cornbread

4 cups cornmeal
⅔ cup all-purpose flour
⅔ cup sugar
1 teaspoon soda
1 teaspoon salt
2 eggs
4 cups buttermilk
2 cups cracklings, chopped

Grease 2 loaf pans, preferably dark or iron loaf pans, as you will get a crustier loaf, which is desirable. (Two small iron skillets could be used instead of loaf pans. If using iron pans, grease well and place in the oven to heat while preheating the oven to 400°. This is a trick used by old-time cooks to ensure a crusty bottom to cornbread.)

In a small bowl sift together the dry ingredients. In a large mixing bowl beat the eggs and add the buttermilk to blend. Add the cracklings and dry ingredients to the egg mixture and stir to blend. Pour into the prepared pans. Bake at 400° for 1 hour for loaf pans, less for skillets, until a cake tester inserted in the center comes out clean. Slice and serve. Excellent served with real butter and with all southern dishes!
Yield: 2 loaves.

Good Coffee Cake

½ cup butter, softened
½ cup shortening
2 cups sugar
2 eggs, slightly beaten
3 cups all-purpose flour
2 teaspoons baking powder
1 teaspoon baking soda
¼ teaspoon salt
1¾ cups buttermilk
2 apples, cored, peeled, and thinly sliced
½ cup all-purpose flour
½ cup sugar
1 teaspoon cinnamon
3 tablespoons butter
½ cup pecans, chopped

In a large mixing bowl cream ½ cup of butter, ½ cup of shortening, and 2 cups of sugar with an electric mixer until light and fluffy. Add the eggs and blend. In a medium mixing bowl sift together 3 cups of flour, the baking powder, baking soda, and salt. Alternately add the flour mixture and buttermilk to the creamed mixture. Pour half the batter in a greased and floured 13 x 9-inch baking pan. Arrange the apple slices over the batter. Pour the remaining batter over the apples.

In a small bowl combine the remaining flour, sugar, and cinnamon. Cut 3 tablespoons of butter into the flour mixture with a pastry cutter. Stir in the nuts and sprinkle the topping over the batter. Bake at 350° for 45 minutes. Cool slightly and cut into squares to serve.
Yield: 15 servings.

Cheesy Cornbread Muffins

2 cups milk
¾ cup cornmeal
2 tablespoons butter
½ cup grated Cheddar cheese
1 cup all-purpose flour
3 teaspoons baking powder
3 tablespoons sugar
1 teaspoon salt
3 eggs, well beaten

In a medium saucepan combine the milk and cornmeal and cook to boiling. Add the butter and cook over low heat for 6 minutes, stirring constantly. Add the cheese and remove the pan from the heat. Let the mixture cool. In a medium bowl stir together the flour, baking powder, sugar, and salt. Add the dry ingredients and eggs to the cornmeal mixture and mix well. Spoon into greased muffin pans. Bake at 350° for 30 to 35 minutes. Serve with butter.
Yield: 16 muffins.

Buttermilk Pancakes

1¼ cups self-rising flour, sifted
½ teaspoon baking soda
1 egg
1¼ cups buttermilk
3 tablespoons vegetable oil

In a small bowl combine the dry ingredients. In a medium bowl beat the egg and whisk in the buttermilk and oil. Stir in the dry ingredients. The batter will be slightly lumpy. Heat a griddle or skillet and grease lightly. Drop the batter by ¼ cupful onto the hot griddle. Turn the pancakes when the tops are covered with bubbles and they are brown on the bottom. Brown on the other side. Serve hot with butter and warm syrup.
Yield: 8 to 10 pancakes.

Fruit Bread

1 cup raisins
¼ cup Jack Daniel's Whiskey
2 cups all-purpose flour
1 teaspoon baking soda
½ teaspoon salt
½ cup butter, softened
1 cup sugar
2 large eggs, beaten
3 medium ripe bananas, mashed
1 large apple, cored, peeled, and chopped
½ cup pecans, chopped
1 teaspoon vanilla extract

In a small bowl soak the raisins in Jack Daniel's Whiskey overnight to soften.
    Grease and flour a 9 x 5 x 3-inch loaf pan. In a medium bowl sift together the flour, baking soda, and salt. In a large bowl cream

the butter and sugar with an electric mixer. Add the eggs and stir in the bananas, apple, pecans, and vanilla. Add the dry ingredients and stir to mix well. Pour the batter into the prepared pan. Bake at 350° for 1 hour or until a cake tester inserted in the center comes out clean. Cool before slicing.
Yield: 1 loaf.

Streusel-Berry Muffins

¼ cup brown sugar
¼ cup all-purpose flour
2 tablespoons butter, melted
¼ cup pecans, chopped
1½ cups all-purpose flour
½ cup sugar
2 teaspoons baking powder
½ cup milk
½ cup butter, melted
1 egg, beaten
1 cup fresh raspberries (or frozen whole
  berries)

In a small bowl combine the brown sugar and ¼ cup of flour. Stir in 2 tablespoons of melted butter and pecans. Set the bowl aside.

In a medium mixing bowl combine the remaining flour, sugar, and baking powder. In a large mixing bowl beat together the milk, butter, and egg. Stir in the flour mixture just until moistened. Spoon half of the batter into greased (or paper-lined) muffin cups. Divide the raspberries among the cups, then top with the remaining batter. Sprinkle the reserved streusel topping over the batter. Bake at 375° for 15 to 20 minutes. Remove the muffins from the pan and serve warm with butter.
Yield: 12 muffins.

Sweet Potato Waffles

½ cup sweet potatoes, cooked and mashed
3 eggs, beaten
1½ cups milk
2 tablespoons butter, melted
1 cup all-purpose flour, sifted
½ teaspoon salt
2 teaspoons baking powder
2 tablespoons sugar
¼ teaspoon nutmeg

In a large bowl combine the potatoes, eggs, milk, and butter; blend well. Sift together the flour, salt, baking powder, sugar, and nutmeg. Gently stir the dry ingredients into the potato mixture and blend only until combined. Pour onto a heated waffle iron. Serve the waffles with Hot Brown Sugar Sauce.
Yield: 4 to 6 waffles.

Hot Brown Sugar Sauce

1 cup brown sugar
½ cup water
1 egg, beaten
3 tablespoons Jack Daniel's Whiskey
Dash salt

In a small saucepan combine the sugar and water, and heat to boiling. Cook for 5 minutes. In a heat-resistant bowl whisk the egg slightly. Pour the hot syrup in a thin stream over the egg while whisking until thickened. Add the Jack Daniel's Whiskey and salt. Serve hot over waffles or pancakes.
Yield: 1½ cups.

Fancy-Dressed French Toast

4 eggs, beaten
½ cup milk
½ cup frozen lemonade, thawed
¼ teaspoon salt
8 tablespoons butter, divided
8 slices day-old bread

In a wide shallow bowl beat the eggs, milk, lemonade, and salt. For each slice, melt 1 tablespoon of butter in a skillet. Dip the bread slices in the egg mixture, turn and coat the other side. Cook the slices in butter, browning on both sides. Serve with Fancy Fruit Sauce.

Fancy Fruit Sauce

1½ cups strawberries, sliced
3 tablespoons sugar
1 8¼-ounce can pineapple chunks, undrained
1 tablespoon butter
1 tablespoon cornstarch
Confectioner's sugar

In a medium bowl sprinkle the strawberries with sugar. In a small saucepan combine the pineapple and butter and heat. Dissolve the cornstarch in a little cold water and add it to the hot pineapple. Cook until bubbly and thick. Remove the pan from the heat and add the strawberries.

To serve, sprinkle each slice of French Toast with confectioners' sugar and then spoon sauce over all.
Yield: 4 servings.

Dew Drop Biscuits

1¾ cups sifted all-purpose flour
3 teaspoons baking powder
½ teaspoon salt
5 tablespoons shortening (or lard)
1 cup milk

In a medium bowl sift together the dry ingredients. Cut in the shortening with a pastry cutter until the mixture looks like coarse cornmeal. Add the milk and stir for 1 minute. Drop the dough by spoonfuls into greased muffin tins. Bake at 450° for 12 to 15 minutes, or until lightly browned.
Yield: 24 biscuits.

Sweet Little Biscuits

3 cups all-purpose flour
⅓ cup sugar
1 tablespoon baking powder
½ teaspoon baking soda
½ teaspoon salt
¾ cup butter
1 cup buttermilk
Milk

In a large bowl stir together the dry ingredients. Cut in the butter with a pastry blender until crumbly. Add the buttermilk and stir until moistened. Turn the dough onto a lightly floured bread board and knead lightly until smooth. Roll the dough to ½-inch thickness and cut with a small biscuit cutter. Place on an ungreased baking sheet. Brush lightly with milk. Bake at 400° for 12 to 15 minutes, or until lightly browned.
Yield: 3 dozen biscuits.

The Farmers Bank

From Miss Mary's memoirs: "My father was one of the first stockholders in this bank. In fact, Dan Evans was the first man to own stock in this bank when it started. His certificate is Number One. This stock has been in the Evans family all these years. M. L. Parks was the first generation to have made deposits in this bank. We now have six generations that have made deposits."

Photo by Hope Powell

Mary Ruth Hall

"**I** CAME TO LIVE at Miss Mary Bobo's Boarding House in September 1949. There were no apartments to rent in the town of Lynchburg, so I became the only female boarder in the house. I paid $12.50 per week for room and board—and board was three meals a day."

Mary Ruth Hall, now one of the lovely hostesses at the boarding house

When Mary Ruth Hall moved to Lynchburg to accept the position of county extension agent, her friends thought her very lucky to be living in a house that often had six men in residence. However, it was more like having six dads or granddads, instead of six would-be suitors, because they all looked out for her.

Most of the rooms were shared by two people. Miss Mary rented out five rooms to boarders and kept one for transients. Mary Ruth and Mr. Tom, president of the bank, and Will Parks, owner of the Ford dealership, each had private rooms. For a time while the Methodist parsonage was being repaired, the minister, his wife, and their three children rented one of the rooms. Each room was outfitted with a washstand, bowl, and pitcher. With only one bathroom, this minimized the length of time each boarder spent in the bath.

Mary Ruth went to work later than the men, so when Miss Mary rang the breakfast bell, Mary Ruth was able to take her turn in the bathroom while the men ate.

Miss Mary served a typical Tennessee country breakfast to her boarders. Dinner, the noon meal, was the main meal of the day, and there were always at least twelve at the table. In addition to her boarders, some local folks came just for the food—and there was always plenty.

Miss Mary kept a vegetable garden. If a lot of people came for dinner, she had groceries close at hand. Supper was the light meal of the day: soup, stew, hash, or leftovers from dinner, with hot bread and dessert.

In the days before television, Miss Mary played the piano in the evening while the boarders relaxed and listened in the parlor. Miss Mary was very good on the piano and loved to play classical and semi-classical music. When her granddaughter, Joan, became a teenager, she purchased some popular sheet music, and Miss Mary learned to play those also.

Room, three meals a day, and entertainment, all for $12.50 per week. Imagine!

The Boarding House Spoon Bread

4 eggs, separated
2 cups milk
3 tablespoons butter
1 cup cornmeal
1 teaspoon baking powder
½ teaspoon salt
¼ teaspoon cream of tartar

In a small mixing bowl beat the egg yolks with an electric mixer at high speed until thick and light. Set them aside.

In a saucepan over medium heat combine the milk and butter. When hot, stir in the cornmeal, baking powder, and salt. When the batter thickens, remove the pan from the heat and gradually beat in the egg yolks. Set the pan aside.

In a medium bowl beat the egg whites with cream of tartar until stiff. Gently fold the batter into the whites and pour into a greased 2-quart baking dish. Bake at 375° for 35 minutes, or until a knife inserted in the center comes out clean. Serve immediately with lots of butter.
Yield: 6 servings.

Raisin Biscuits

2 cups self-rising flour, sifted
1 teaspoon cinnamon
¼ cup shortening
1 cup raisins
⅞ cup buttermilk (1 cup less 2 tablespoons)
1 cup confectioners' sugar
1 tablespoon milk
½ teaspoon vanilla extract

In a medium mixing bowl combine the flour and cinnamon. Cut the shortening into the flour mixture with a pastry blender or two knives until the mixture resembles coarse crumbs. Stir in the raisins. Add the buttermilk and stir with a fork only until the dough leaves the sides of the bowl. Turn the dough onto a lightly floured bread board and knead gently just until smooth. Roll out to ½-inch thickness. Cut into rounds with a floured 3-inch cutter. Place on a greased baking sheet. Bake at 450° for 10 to 12 minutes, or until golden brown.

In a small bowl combine the confectioners' sugar, milk, and vanilla. Stir until smooth. Spoon over the hot biscuits and serve.
Yield: 12 to 14 biscuits.

Party Puffs

1 cup water
½ cup butter
1 cup all-purpose flour
4 eggs

In a small saucepan combine the water and butter and bring to a boil. Stir in the flour and cook until the mixture forms a ball, stirring constantly. Remove from the heat. Beat in the eggs, one at a time. Drop by the teaspoonful onto a greased baking sheet. Bake at 450° for 15 minutes. Reduce the heat to 300° and continue to bake for 30 to 40 minutes, or until golden brown. Cool. Cut in two, remove the insides, and fill with chicken salad or your favorite filling.
Yield: 12 to 14 puffs.

Frisky Fritters

2 cups all-purpose flour
1 tablespoon baking powder
½ teaspoon salt
3 tablespoons sugar
2 eggs, well beaten
1 cup milk
2 cups tart apples, peeled and chopped
1 teaspoon cinnamon
Oil
½ cup sugar
¼ cup Jack Daniel's Whiskey

In a medium mixing bowl sift together the flour, baking powder, salt, and 3 tablespoons of sugar. In a small bowl combine the eggs and milk, then gradually stir the mixture into the dry ingredients. Refrigerate the batter for 2 hours.

Stir in the apples and cinnamon. In a skillet heat 1 to 2 inches of oil. Drop by the tablespoonful into hot oil and fry until golden brown. In a shallow bowl mix ½ cup of sugar with the Jack Daniel's Whiskey, roll fritters to coat while hot, and serve.
Yield: 8 servings.

Potato Rolls

½ cup shortening
2 cups warm milk
½ cup sugar
½ cup mashed potatoes
¼ cup warm water
3 packages yeast
2 eggs, slightly beaten
½ teaspoon soda
2 teaspoons baking powder
2 teaspoons salt
6 cups flour

Stir together first four ingredients and set aside. Dissolve yeast into warm water and add to other warm ingredients. Sift flour with soda, baking powder, and salt. Stir eggs into warm ingredients, adding flour while stirring. Let dough rise, covered, in the refrigerator. Punch down and knead on board. Roll dough out on board and then shape into rolls. Bake at 375° until golden brown.

Note: Dough will keep in refrigerator for one week covered, and you can remove as much as you wish to bake at a time.
Yield: 3 dozen rolls.

Entrées

Boarding House Meat Loaf

This meat loaf has been a favorite with Miss Mary's guests for so many years. For pleasing your guests or family, this is a real winner!

1½ pounds ground beef
¾ cup uncooked oatmeal
1½ teaspoons salt
¼ cup onions, chopped
¼ cup bell pepper, chopped
¼ cup catsup
2 eggs, beaten
Meat Loaf Sauce

Grease a 9 x 3-inch loaf pan. In a large bowl combine all the ingredients and form into a loaf. Place into the prepared pan. Bake at 350° for 1 hour. Pour off the juice and bake about 10 minutes longer. Place on a platter and cover with sauce.

Meat Loaf Sauce

¾ cup catsup
2 tablespoons onion, chopped
2 tablespoons bell pepper, chopped
¼ cup brown sugar, firmly packed

In a small saucepan simmer the sauce over low heat until the onion and pepper are tender.
Yield: 6 to 8 servings.

Our Own Country Steak

1 pound round steak
1 teaspoon seasoned meat tenderizer
1 cup all-purpose flour
¼ teaspoon black pepper
Vegetable oil
1 cup water
1 10¾-ounce can cream of mushroom soup
2 medium onions, sliced

Cut the steak into serving-size pieces. Combine the meat tenderizer, flour, and pepper. Dredge the steak in the flour mixture. Heat the oil in a heavy skillet (1 inch deep to cover the steak). Place the steak pieces in hot oil; brown on both sides. Remove the steak from the oil. Pour off the oil from the skillet. To the skillet add the water, soup, and onions and stir to blend. Add the steak, cover, and simmer over low heat for 1 hour. More water may be added, if needed.
Yield: 4 servings.

Miss Mary with Friends and Boarders

Miss Mary with friends in front of the boarding house, about 1967. (L-R) Mrs. Laura Mae Parker, a permanent boarder who lived here until her death in her nineties; Jeanie Motlow, widow of Reagor Motlow, a former state senator and oldest son of Lem Motlow; Nell Fanning, Miss Mary, and Louise Crutcher, Miss Mary's daughter; Mary B. Parkes and Catherine Sorrells, the daughter of Mrs. Laura Mae Parker, another widow who boarded at the house during the week and worked at the distillery as a hostess (on weekends she went to her home in Petersburg).

Photo courtesy of Joan Crutcher Ferguson

Swiss Steak

4 tablespoons oil (or bacon drippings)
1 1½-pound round steak, cut into serving size
 pieces
Flour
Salt and pepper
2 large onions, peeled and sliced
1 16-ounce can stewed tomatoes
½ cup water
1 tablespoon Worcestershire sauce

In a large skillet heat oil over medium heat. Dredge the steak in flour and liberally sprinkle with salt and pepper. Brown in hot oil. Combine the onions, tomatoes, water, and Worcestershire sauce. As the steak browns, remove to 2-quart baking dish. Spoon the tomato mixture over the steak. Cover and bake at 350° for one hour and 15 minutes; add water if necessary. Steak will be fork tender. Serve with sauce spooned over steak, and mashed potatoes if desired.
Yield: 6 to 8 servings.

Tenderloin Tips

¼ cup butter
2 pounds beef tenderloin tips, thinly sliced
2 teaspoons salt
1 cup mushrooms, sliced
¼ cup onion, chopped
1 clove garlic, minced
½ cup burgundy wine
½ cup Jack Daniel's Whiskey
1 cup canned tomatoes, crushed
2 cubes beef bouillon
2 teaspoons sugar
Mashed potatoes

In a large skillet melt the butter and sauté the meat quickly, half at a time, until browned. Add the salt, mushrooms, onion, and garlic and simmer for several minutes, adding extra butter if needed. Add the wine, Jack Daniel's Whiskey, tomatoes, bouillon cubes, and sugar. Simmer for 30 minutes or until tender. Serve on a platter with mashed potatoes.
Yield: 4 servings.

Miz Dill's Pot Roast

2 pounds beef chuck roast
1 teaspoon salt
½ teaspoon pepper
2 teaspoons seasoned meat tenderizer
¼ cup all-purpose flour
1 large onion, sliced
1 bell pepper, sliced
1 cup water

Rinse and pat the roast dry. In a shallow bowl mix the salt, pepper, meat tenderizer, and flour. Press the seasonings onto all sides of the roast. Place the roast in a dutch oven; add the vegetables and water. Cover and bake at 350° for 2 hours. Cut in pieces and serve.
 Note: This roast makes its own gravy, so it is perfect for those hostesses who hate to make gravy. At Miss Mary's this roast is served on a platter with cooked carrots and the gravy over all.
Yield: 6 servings.

Old No. 7 Tennessee Beef Brisket

1 4- to 6-pound beef brisket
¼ cup Jack Daniel's Whiskey
¼ cup soy sauce
¼ cup catsup (optional)
¼ cup brown sugar
1 medium onion, finely chopped
2 tablespoons Dijon mustard
2 cloves garlic, minced
Black pepper to taste
Dash Worcestershire sauce

Trim the external fat from the beef brisket to ¼ inch. Place the brisket in a large plastic storage container or glass baking dish. In a large measuring cup combine the remaining ingredients. Add enough water to make 2 cups of marinade. Pour the mixture over the brisket. Seal or cover tightly and refrigerate for 8 hours or overnight. Remove the brisket and place in a foil roasting pan. Pour the marinade over the brisket. Cover with heavy duty foil and seal tightly. Bake at 275° for 4 to 5 hours. Remove the brisket from the pan. Skim the fat from pan drippings. Reheat and serve with the brisket.

Note: If you desire a grilled flavor to your meat, after baking you may place brisket over moderate coals, fat side down. Close the lid on the grill and cook for about 30 minutes. For hickory-smoke flavor, soak hickory chips in water for 30 minutes and sprinkle over moderate coals just before grilling the meat.

Yield: 12 to 18 servings.

Farmer's Country-Fried Steak

When the American Festival Cafe in New York City did a tribute to Miss Mary Bobo's Boarding House and served her typical boarding house meals for two months, this was one of the recipes they chose to offer. It was a big success. Many of their guests had never eaten country-fried steak. To those who live in the South, this seems unthinkable!

2 pounds round steak
½ teaspoon salt
½ teaspoon pepper
½ cup all-purpose flour
1 tablespoon vegetable oil
1 onion, chopped
1 cup chicken stock or water
1 cup buttermilk
1 cup Cheddar cheese, shredded

Cut the steak into 6 to 8 serving pieces. Pound with a kitchen mallet or the rim of a saucer until thin. Spinkle with salt and pepper; dust with flour. In a skillet heat the oil and sear the meat until evenly brown on all sides. Add the onion and cook for several minutes, until limp. In a bowl combine the chicken stock and buttermilk. Pour the mixture over the meat. Stir to loosen the crust from the bottom of the skillet. Cover and cook over medium low heat until the meat is tender, 45 to 50 minutes. Add the cheese and stir into the gravy. This is delicious over rice or biscuits.

Yield: 6 to 8 servings.

DURING WORLD WAR II, the boarding house was run as the Bobo Hotel. Camp Forest was nearby, and Lynchburg had many soldiers in town on maneuvers. The officers, who loved to eat at the boarding house, had such privileges restricted to officers only. Officers wanted to be able to drink in the dining room, but Miss Mary had a long-standing rule that prohibited drinking in her house. She said no to the generals just like she did to any other person requesting permission to drink in her establishment. In her house even the general had to do as he was told!

Saturday's Stew

2 tablespoons all-purpose flour
2 teaspoons salt
1 teaspoon pepper
2 pounds round steak, cut into 1-inch cubes (or use stew meat)
2 tablespoons bacon drippings or vegetable oil
½ cup Jack Daniel's Whiskey
2 16-ounce cans stewed tomatoes
2 10½-ounce cans beef broth
½ pound small whole onions (or frozen)
½ pound carrots, cut into 1-inch pieces
8 medium new potatoes, washed and cut in half

In a bowl mix the flour, salt, and pepper. Roll the meat in the flour to coat well. In a dutch oven brown the meat in bacon drippings. Add Jack Daniel's Whiskey, tomatoes, and broth and bring the mixture to a boil. Reduce the heat and simmer for 2 hours (a cup of water may be added during the cooking time to make more juice for stew). Add the onions, carrots, and potatoes and cook until tender.

Note: An old-fashioned way of serving stew is to spoon into bowls and pass a bottle of catsup so guests can add as desired.

Serve with cornbread or crackers.
Yield: 8 servings.

Country Goulash

1 pound beef stew meat
1 pound pork, cut into cubes
6 small onions, peeled and quartered
4 tablespoons bacon drippings (or shortening)
Salt and pepper
1 clove garlic, minced
3 tablespoons paprika
1 tablespoon marjoram
¼ cup fresh parsley, chopped
1 16-ounce can stewed tomatoes
1 8-ounce can tomato sauce
5 potatoes, peeled and cut in chunks
1½ cups carrots, sliced

In a large stew pot brown the meats in hot oil. Stir in the onions and salt and pepper generously. Add the remaining ingredients with two or three cups water, bring to a boil, then reduce heat and simmer for one hour.
Yield: 8 servings.

Black Label Sirloin Roast

1 4-pound beef sirloin roast
2 cups catsup
¼ cup Jack Daniel's Whiskey
2 tablespoons Worcestershire sauce
½ cup dark brown sugar
¼ cup lemon juice

Place the roast on a rack in a shallow roasting pan. Combine the remaining ingredients in a saucepan and heat until the sugar melts. Baste the roast with the sauce. Bake at 350° for 2 hours for rare (140° on meat thermometer) or 2½ hours for medium (160°). Baste frequently during cooking time.
Yield: 8 to 10 servings.

Pot Roast and Noodles

This was a typical Sunday dinner, served with salad and the usual vegetable side dishes. The meat could be prepared the day before, and while the noodles were cooking on Sunday, the meat and sauce would be reheated—delicious!

1 4- to 5-pound pot roast
3 tablespoons bacon drippings (or oil)
1 16-ounce can whole berry cranberry sauce
1 16-ounce can tomato sauce
1 cup water
2 envelopes onion soup mix
Hot cooked noodles

In a large dutch oven, sear the roast in hot oil. Combine the cranberry sauce, tomato sauce, water, and soup mix. Pour over the browned roast. Cover. Bake at 350° for 2½ hours or until tender.

If cooked the day before, cover and refrigerate. The next day, skim any fat from the drippings, slice the meat, and return to the pot. Reheat with the sauce in the pot. Arrange cooked noodles on a platter with sliced meat over top. Spoon the delicious pan gravy over all.
Yield: 6 to 8 servings.

Liver and Onions

Throughout the South the cooking oil of choice was bacon drippings or lard because of the availability and also the flavor it imparted to the dishes. Today's health-conscious chefs use cholesterol-free fat, which is an acceptable substitute for bacon drippings or lard. However, by doing this you also miss the way things used to taste!

1 pound beef liver
¼ cup all-purpose flour
Salt and pepper
2 tablespoons bacon drippings (or cooking oil)
2 onions, peeled and thinly sliced
1 cup water, divided
1 tablespoon all-purpose flour

Cut the liver into ¼-inch slices. Coat the slices with flour and season generously with salt and pepper. In a skillet brown the meat in the bacon drippings. Add the onion slices and half the water. Cover and lower the heat to simmer. Cook for 15 minutes, or until the liver is tender. Remove the liver from the skillet and whisk in flour. Add the remaining water. Return the liver to the gravy and cook until the gravy is thickened.
Yield: 4 servings.

THE MAN WHO MAKES THE ICED TEA at Lynchburg's hotel says it's better because it's made with Jack Daniel's limestone water.

Folks who take lunch at our hotel always have something good to say about the tea. And George Gant, who serves it, tells them it's because he makes it with water from Jack Daniel's limestone spring. Well, we know it makes a difference in whiskey. You see, it runs fresh from our cave at 56° year-round, and it's completely iron-free. Iron is murderous to whiskey. And from what George says, it doesn't do tea much good either.

CHARCOAL
MELLOWED
◊
DROP
◊
BY DROP

© 1964, Jack Daniel Distillery, Lem Motlow, Prop., Inc.

TENNESSEE WHISKEY • 90 PROOF BY CHOICE • DISTILLED AND BOTTLED BY JACK DANIEL DISTILLERY • LYNCHBURG (POP. 384), TENN.

Mouse, for more than forty years a part of the boarding house hospitality

George Gant was six or seven years old when he came to the boarding house. Everyone called him Mouse. The Bobos tried to get him to go to school, but he refused. He lived in the tenant house out back. Mouse is a part of the tradition of this establishment and is affectionately remembered as an important part of the wonderful staff that served the boarding house. Mouse waited and cleared the tables, made fires in the wood stoves, and was generally considered the major-domo of the house.

The football team at Moore County High School made Mouse its official water boy and gave him a school sweater. He was extremely proud of this. He lived here until his health in later years forced him to live with an aunt who cared for him. Mouse was a friend to everyone. Miss Mary's children, grandchildren, and great-grandchildren credit Mouse with helping raise them, earning him high esteem and deep affection.

Photo courtesy of Joan Crutcher Ferguson

Baked Chicken with Cream

12 chicken breast halves
2 cups sour cream
2 teaspoons Worcestershire sauce
Juice of 1 lemon
2 ribs celery, minced
1 medium onion, minced
1 clove garlic, minced
½ teaspoon dried red pepper flakes
1 teaspoon salt
1½ cups cornbread crumbs
1 teaspoon poultry seasoning
½ cup melted butter, divided

Butter a 13 x 9-inch baking dish. Wash the chicken breasts and set aside to drain on paper towels.

In a medium mixing bowl combine the sour cream, Worcestershire sauce, lemon juice, celery, onion, garlic, red pepper flakes, and salt. Dip the chicken breasts in the sour cream mixture and place in the prepared dish. Pour the remaining sour cream mixture over the chicken breasts. Cover and refrigerate for at least 1 hour.

In a small bowl combine the cornbread crumbs and poultry seasoning. Set the bowl aside.

When ready to bake the chicken, top with seasoned cornbread crumbs and drizzle with ¼ cup of melted butter. Cover with foil. Bake at 350° for 45 minutes. Uncover and drizzle the remaining butter over the top. Continue to bake for 15 minutes longer, or until the topping is browned and crusty.
Yield: 12 servings.

Chicken Squares with Mushroom Sauce

This is an especially good dish for brunch.

3 cups cooked chicken, chopped
1 cup cooked rice
2 cups soft bread crumbs
½ cup celery, finely chopped
1 2-ounce jar diced pimientos
4 eggs, beaten
1 teaspoon salt
½ teaspoon poultry seasoning
2 cups chicken broth

Grease a 9-inch square baking dish. In a large bowl combine the chicken, rice, bread crumbs, celery, and pimiento. Add the eggs, salt, poultry seasoning, and broth. Stir well. Pour into the prepared dish. Bake at 325° for 40 to 50 minutes or until set. Cut into squares and serve with Mushroom Sauce.

Mushroom Sauce

½ pound fresh mushrooms, sliced
3 tablespoons butter
1 cup medium white sauce (or 1 can cream of mushroom soup)

In a saucepan melt the butter and sauté the mushrooms until tender. Add the white sauce and heat until bubbly.
Yield: 8 to 10 servings.

Miss Mary's Famous Chicken with Pastry

Velma Waggoner, the boarding house's singing cook, is the lady who has prepared this recipe for many years. It is always a crowd pleaser and is one of the recipes most requested by the guests.

1 2½- to 3-pound chicken
3 cups water
1 large onion
1 rib celery
1 teaspoon salt
¼ cup all-purpose flour
¼ cup water
Salt and pepper to taste
2 cups all-purpose flour
1 teaspoon salt
¾ cup shortening (Miss Mary's uses lard)
¼ cup cold water

In a large pot combine the chicken, 3 cups of water, onion, celery, and 1 teaspoon of salt. Cook over medium heat until tender. When tender, remove the chicken from the broth and debone. Cut into large chunks. Grease a 9 x 12-inch baking dish. Place the chicken in the dish. Remove the celery and onion from the broth. Blend ¼ cup of flour with ¼ cup of water to make a smooth paste and gradually whisk the paste into the simmering broth to make gravy. Cook for 5 to 10 minutes, or until thickened. Season with salt and pepper. Pour enough gravy over the chicken to just cover.

In a large bowl combine 2 cups of flour and 1 teaspoon of salt. Cut in shortening with a pastry blender or fork until the mixture resembles cornmeal. Sprinkle in the cold water and mix until the dough holds together and will form a ball. Roll out on a floured board to about ¼ inch thickness. Cut into strips and place over the chicken. Bake at 375° until the pastry has browned.

Note: This may be served in the same baking dish in which it is prepared. However, at Miss Mary's the platter is covered with gravy and the chicken with pastry spooned over the gravy.

Yield: 6 servings.

Smothered Chicken Breasts

8 large chicken breast halves
1 cup all-purpose flour
Salt and pepper
½ cup bacon drippings (or vegetable oil)
3 tablespoons all-purpose flour
4 cups chicken stock, heated (or canned stock)
Salt and pepper, to taste
1 4-ounce jar mushroom slices

Dredge the chicken breasts in 1 cup of flour and sprinkle generously with salt and pepper. In a large heavy skillet heat the fat until hot. Brown the chicken breasts and then place them in a 9 x 13-inch baking dish. Reserve ¼ cup of drippings, and discard the remainder. Return the reserved drippings to the hot skillet. When the drippings are hot again, sprinkle in 3 tablespoons of flour, stirring constantly. Brown flour but do not burn. Slowly add the stock, stirring until well blended. Simmer over low heat for 4 to 5 minutes. Stir in salt and pepper and the mushroom slices with juice. Pour the gravy over the chicken pieces. Cover the baking dish. Bake at 325° for 1 hour.

Yield: 8 servings.

Fancy Chicken

1 2½- to 3-pound chicken, cut into pieces (or 4
  chicken breasts)
Salt and pepper to taste
2 tablespoons butter
2 tablespoons vegetable oil
½ cup Jack Daniel's Whiskey
6 shallots, chopped (or 1 onion, chopped)
¼ teaspoon powdered thyme
¼ cup minced fresh parsley
¼ cup water
1 cup heavy cream

Sprinkle the chicken with salt and pepper.
In a large skillet heat the butter and oil and
brown the chicken pieces on both sides. Add
the Jack Daniel's Whiskey and carefully
ignite, shaking the skillet until the flames go
out. Add the shallots and cook for 1 minute.
Add the thyme, parsley, and water; cover the
skillet and cook over low heat, turning occasionally, for 25 to 35 minutes. Transfer the
chicken to a warm platter. Add the cream to
the skillet and simmer, stirring until the
sauce thickens. Serve the sauce over the
chicken.
Yield: 4 servings.

Traditional Southern Fried Chicken

1 2- to 2½-pound chicken
2 eggs
1 cup milk
1½ teaspoons salt
1 teaspoon pepper
1½ cups self-rising flour
3 cups lard

Cut the chicken into frying pieces. In a
shallow bowl beat the eggs and then stir in
the milk, salt, and pepper. Soak the chicken
in the milk mixture for 5 to 10 minutes. Roll
the chicken in flour, being sure to completely
cover each piece. Set aside to dry.

In a large cast-iron skillet melt lard over
medium high heat. When the fat is very hot
add the thighs and legs and cook for several
minutes. Add the other pieces, being careful
not to overcrowd the skillet. Continue cooking until the chicken is golden brown on one
side (about 5 minutes). Turn and brown on
the other side. Reduce the heat to medium
low. Cover the pan and cook for 15 minutes.
Turn the pieces, cover, and continue to cook
for 15 minutes longer. Uncover for the last 5
to 10 minutes so the crust will be crisp.
Yield: 4 to 5 servings.

Chicken and Dumplings

1 2½- to 3-pound stewing chicken
1 large onion
2 ribs celery
½ green bell pepper
1 teaspoon salt
8 cups water
2 cups all-purpose flour, sifted
½ teaspoon salt
⅓ cup lard (or shortening)
1 egg
Cold water

In large saucepan combine the chicken, vegetables, 1 teaspoon of salt, and 8 cups of
water. Bring the mixture to a boil. Cover and
reduce the heat to a simmer. Cook for 1 hour
or until tender. Remove the chicken from the
broth and cool. Discard the vegetables and
skim the fat from broth. Bone the chicken,

chop and reserve the meat. Return the broth to a boil.

To make the dumplings, stir together the flour and ½ teaspoon of salt. Cut in the lard with a pastry cutter until crumbly. Beat the egg in a measuring cup and add enough cold water to make a half cup. Add to the flour and stir with a fork until the dough leaves the sides of the bowl. Roll out the dough on a lightly floured board to ⅛-inch thickness. Cut into strips and slowly drop into the boiling broth. Cover and simmer for 15 minutes. Stir several times to prevent the dumplings from sticking together. Just before serving, stir in the chopped chicken to heat through. *Yield: 8 to 10 servings.*

Chicken and Cornbread Casserole

3 cups cornbread, crumbled
2 tablespoons poultry seasoning
1 teaspoon sage
½ cup butter, melted
1½ cups chicken stock (or canned stock)
1 cup sour cream
½ cup mayonnaise
1 4-ounce jar sliced mushrooms with juice
3½ cups cooked chicken, cubed
½ cup onion, peeled and chopped
½ cup celery, diced
¼ teaspoon dried red pepper flakes
Salt to taste

In a large bowl combine the cornbread, poultry seasoning, and sage. Pour the melted butter over the crumbs and stir to blend. Cover the bottom of a 9 x 5-inch glass baking dish with half of the crumbs. Combine the remaining ingredients and spread the mixture over the crumbs. Top with the remaining crumbs. Bake at 325° for 30 to 35 minutes.

Note: Casserole may be topped with 2 cups of shredded sharp Cheddar cheese after first 15 minutes of baking time, if desired. *Yield: 8 to 10 servings.*

BOARDERS' STORIES

Mr. Watts, the monument salesman

MR. WATTS WAS A monument salesman who traveled all the time. When he was in the Lynchburg area, he roomed at Miss Mary's Boarding House. He was fond of her grandchildren, who lived next door. Joan, Miss Mary's granddaughter, had a dog named Brownie. When Brownie was run over by a car and killed, the children buried Brownie in their backyard. Mr. Watts had the workers at Bockman Monument Company in Sparta make a tombstone. It read:

BROWNIE
PET DOG OF JOAN CRUTCHER
KILLED BY AUTO
JUNE 4, 1941
EVERYBODY'S PAL

After her parents died, Joan and her brother sold the family home, and she had the marker moved to her home in Wartrace.

Breakfast at the Boarding House

Because the boarding house no longer takes in roomers, breakfast is not offered today. But for many decades breakfast at Miss Mary Bobo's was a memorable meal. Here, Mr. Tom Motlow, a long-time boarder, sits at the table eating breakfast.

Although the table is set, the other boarders have not yet come to the table. Any minute now, you expect Miss Mary to ring the bell for breakfast. Today, that tradition continues with a ringing bell drawing diners to a scrumptious mid-day meal.

Baked Turkey with Cornbread Dressing

1 10- to 12-pound turkey
1 large onion
1 rib celery
¼ cup butter, softened

Remove the neck, gizzard, heart, and liver from the turkey and reserve them for gravy. Rinse the turkey and pat dry. Rub inside the cavity with salt and insert the onion and celery. Coat the turkey lightly with softened butter. Place in a roaster, cover and bake at 350° for 20 minutes per pound, about 3 to 3½ hours. After baking discard the onion and celery and reserve the broth for the dressing.
Yield: 10 to 12 servings.

Cornbread Dressing

3 eggs, beaten
3 cups self-rising cornmeal
2 cups buttermilk
½ cup bacon drippings or vegetable oil
½ cup celery, chopped
½ cup onion, chopped
1 tablespoon sage
¼ teaspoon black pepper
2 to 3 cups turkey broth (or chicken broth)

Grease a 12-inch skillet. In a large bowl mix the eggs, cornmeal, buttermilk, and bacon drippings and pour into the prepared skillet. Bake at 350° for 20 minutes, until golden brown. Crumble the cornbread into a large bowl. Add the celery, onion, sage, and black pepper to the crumbled cornbread. Stir in 2 or more cups of broth from the turkey, or just enough to moisten. Grease a 13 x 9-inch glass dish. Pour the batter into the baking dish. Bake at 425° for 35 to 40 minutes, or until golden brown.
Yield: 10 to 12 servings.

Prize Turkey

¼ cup butter
1 pound mushrooms, stemmed and sliced
½ cup celery, finely chopped
1 small onion, finely chopped
4 tablespoons flour
1½ cups half and half
2 cups cooked turkey, cut in chunks
½ teaspoon salt
Pepper
*1 package spaghetti, cooked and cut in small
    pieces*
2 cups Cheddar cheese, grated

In a large skillet melt the butter and sauté mushrooms, celery, and onion. In a cup combine the flour and a small amount of water to make a paste; add to cream and stir into the skillet. Stirring constantly, cook until thick. Add the turkey, salt, and generous sprinkle of freshly ground pepper. Stir cooked spaghetti into the turkey mixture. Place in a 2-quart baking dish and cover with Cheddar cheese. Bake at 350° just until cheese melts.
Yield: 8 servings.

Giblet Gravy

Turkey neck, gizzard, heart, and liver
3 cups water
1 teaspoon salt
6 tablespoons all-purpose flour
½ cup water
3 hard-boiled eggs, sliced
Salt and pepper to taste

In a large saucepan place the turkey parts. Add 3 cups of water and the salt. Cover and cook over medium heat until tender, about 1½ hours. Remove the meat from the broth and discard the neck. Make giblets by chopping the remaining parts and return to broth. Blend the flour with ½ cup of water to form a smooth paste. Stir the paste into the broth. Cook, stirring constantly, until thickened. Add the sliced eggs and season to taste. Serve with the turkey and dressing.
Yield: 3 cups.

Yorkshire Ducks

½ pound ground lean pork
½ pound ground sausage (bulk sausage broken up)
½ pound ground veal
1 egg
1 cup soft bread crumbs
1 small onion, finely chopped
¼ cup water
1 teaspoon sage
Salt and pepper to taste
Steak sauce or catsup

In a large mixing bowl combine the ground meats. In a medium mixing bowl combine the egg, bread crumbs, onion, and water. Add the mixture to the meats with the sage, salt, and pepper. Shape into 6 small loaves and place on a baking pan with dripper insert. Bake at 350° for 40 minutes. Place a generous spoonful of your favorite steak sauce or catsup on top and return to the oven for 5 minutes. Serve with additional steak sauce on the table.
Yield: 6 servings.

Our Famous Pork Ribs

Miss Mary Bobo's has a number of guests who request that they be called when our famous pork ribs are on the menu. The cooks make sure that there is plenty to satisfy these regular guests' appetites!

2 pounds country-style lean pork ribs
1 teaspoon seasoned meat tenderizer
½ teaspoon red pepper flakes
12 to 14 ounces tomato catsup
½ cup onion, grated
Salt

Cut the ribs into serving pieces and sprinkle with meat tenderizer. In a large pot place ribs and add water to cover them. Cover the pot and cook the ribs until tender.

In a small saucepan prepare the sauce by combining the remaining ingredients. Bring to a boil, reduce the heat, and simmer for 15 minutes. Place the ribs in a 3-quart size baking dish. Pour the sauce over the ribs. Bake at 350° for 30 minutes.
Yield: 4 servings.

Fancy Chops

2 tablespoons cooking oil
6 thick cut pork chops
Salt and pepper
1 large onion, sliced
1 lemon, sliced
½ cup firmly packed brown sugar
6 tablespoons ketchup
4 tablespoons Jack Daniel's Whiskey

In a large skillet heat oil and brown the chops over medium heat. Season with salt and pepper generously. When browned, place the chops in a shallow baking dish. Place one onion slice and one lemon slice on top of each chop. Combine remaining ingredients and spoon over the top of each chop. Cover and bake at 350° for 40 minutes. Remove the cover and bake 30 minutes or until done. Spoon basting sauce over the chops occasionally. . . . *Yum!*
Yield: 6 servings.

Cider-Sauced Pork Tenderloin

1 pound pork tenderloin
½ teaspoon black pepper
½ teaspoon sage
½ teaspoon thyme
½ teaspoon ginger
½ teaspoon cinnamon
½ teaspoon salt
1 tablespoon vegetable oil
1 onion, minced
1 large apple, peeled and chopped
½ cup apple cider

Slice the pork crosswise into 8 medallions. Mix the seasonings together and coat the pork slices. In a large skillet heat the oil and sear the pork on both sides until brown. Remove the pork to a platter and cover to keep warm. To the oil in the skillet add the onion and apple and sauté until golden. Add the cider to the skillet and heat to simmer. Place the pork slices in simmering liquid, cover, and simmer for 5 to 10 minutes. Serve immediately.
Yield: 4 servings.

Southern Pork Roast

2½ pounds pork loin roast
Seasoned meat tenderizer
Lemon pepper
Salt
1 large onion, sliced
1 bell pepper, sliced
2 ribs celery
1 cup water

Rub the roast generously with seasonings and place in a greased dutch oven. Lay the vegetables on the top and around the sides and add the water. Cover and bake at 350° for 1½ to 2 hours. Cool for 20 minutes before slicing.

Note: Miss Mary's serves this with Cornbread Dressing (see page 93), and then we make a brown gravy with the drippings from the roast to serve with the roast and dressing. It is *goooood* eating!
Yield: 8 to 10 servings.

Mrs. Bobo's Boarding House, Lynchburg, Tn.

MRS. BOBO'S MENU

Mrs. Bobo said this would give you some idea of what she serves. But don't go expecting to get exactly what's listed here. Mrs. Bobo doesn't know herself what she's going to fix until she gets up and does some puttering around the kitchen.

◆ MEATS ◆
(at least two)

Mrs. Bobo's Southern Fried Chicken	Beef Roast
Fried Pork Tenderloin	Pork Chops Country Style
Fresh River Catfish & Hush Puppies	Baked Hen & Dressing
Country Ham & Red-Eye Gravy	

◆ VEGETABLES AND THINGS ◆
(at least seven)

Uncle Jack's Cheese Grits	Fresh Cucumber Relish
Fried Okra	Sliced Garden Tomatoes
Texas Red Hot	Stewed Tomatoes
White Beans & Ham Bits	Pears Baked in Sugar & Butter
Egg & Asparagus Casserole	Scalloped Potatoes
Deviled Eggs	Candied Sweet Potatoes
Old-Fashioned Green Beans	Black-Eyed Peas
Baked Apples	Miss Dill's Scalloped Oysters
Turnip Greens with Hog Jowl	Country Fried Corn
Mr. Lem's Country Squash Casserole	Macaroni & Cheese
Southern Fruit Salad	Moore Country Cabbage Slaw

◆ DESSERTS ◆

Cumberland Mt. Chocolate Pie	Rebel Pecan Pie
Japanese Fruit Pie	Woodforth Pudding
Fresh Fruit Pies	Caramel Cake & Ice Cream
Fresh Fruit Cobblers	Mary Lou's Chess Pie

And, of course, platters and platters of hot, fresh-baked corn bread or biscuits.

Menu, circa 1970

A circa 1970 dinner menu circulated to tour companies desiring to bring their groups to Miss Mary Bobo's Boarding House for dinner. Groups touring the distillery could enjoy the boarding house fare, a unique experience for every visitor.

Pork in Pastry

2 pounds ground pork tenderloin
¼ pound ham, ground (or cut into small cubes)
2 potatoes, cooked and diced
1 onion, chopped
2 eggs, beaten
1 teaspoon Worcestershire sauce
1 teaspoon cinnamon
¼ teaspoon cloves
¼ teaspoon allspice
Pastry for 9-inch double-crust deep-dish pie

In a large mixing bowl combine the ground meats, vegetables, eggs, and seasonings. Mix well. Line a 9-inch deep-dish pie plate with pastry. Spoon in the meat mixture. Top with the remaining pastry and press with a fork to seal. Pierce with a knife to vent. Bake at 350° for 45 minutes or until done. Cool slightly, cut into wedges, and serve.
Yield: 8 servings.

Kraut and Smoked Sausage

⅓ cup chopped onion
3 tablespoons bacon drippings
1 cup beer
1 cup water
2 tablespoons cornstarch
1 heaping tablespoon spicy mustard
2 tablespoons molasses
1 teaspoon caraway seed
½ teaspoon ground allspice
½ teaspoon whole black peppercorns
1 large rutabaga, peeled and shredded
1 pound fully cooked smoked sausage, cut in 2½-inch pieces
2 apples, chopped
1 16-ounce jar sauerkraut, drained and rinsed

In a large stock pot sauté the onion in bacon drippings. Stir in the beer. Combine the water and cornstarch and stir to blend until smooth. Add the cornstarch mixture to the pan with the mustard, molasses, and spices. Cook and stir until it is bubbly and begins to thicken. Add the rutabaga, cover, and cook for 10 minutes. Add the remaining ingredients, cover, and cook until the apples are tender, about 15 minutes.
Yield: 6 servings.

Country Ham and Chicken Pie

1 3-pound stewing chicken
1 teaspoon salt
1 teaspoon allspice
1 teaspoon black peppercorns
1 bay leaf
3 carrots, cut in ½-inch pieces
3 ribs celery, cut in ½-inch pieces
3 large onions, peeled and cut in chunks
1 pound country ham, cut into chunks
4 hard-boiled eggs, sliced
Unbaked pastry for double-crust 9-inch pie
¼ cup butter
¼ cup all-purpose flour
⅓ cup Jack Daniel's Whiskey
2 tablespoons lemon juice
¼ teaspoon mace
¼ teaspoon dried red pepper flakes
2 egg yolks
1 egg, beaten

In a large dutch oven cover the stewing chicken with water and add 1 teaspoon of salt, the allspice, peppercorns, and bay leaf. Bring the water to a boil. Add the carrots, celery, and onions, cover, and simmer for 30 minutes. Remove the chicken from the broth. Remove the vegetables and set them aside. Strain the broth. Remove and discard the skin and bones from the chicken and cut the meat into chunks. Line the bottom and sides of a 12 x 8-inch baking dish with pastry. Place the chicken, carrots, celery, onion, ham, and sliced eggs over the pastry.

In a medium saucepan melt the butter and stir in the flour and 1 teaspoon of salt. Gradually add 2 cups of the reserved broth, the Jack Daniel's Whiskey, lemon juice, mace, and red pepper flakes. Cook, stirring constantly, until thickened. In a small bowl beat the egg yolks. Add a small amount of the hot liquid to the egg yolks, then slowly stir the egg yolks into the sauce. Cook, stirring constantly, until thickened. Do not boil. Pour the sauce over the ham, chicken, and vegetables. Roll out the top pastry to cover the casserole, leaving an overhang of ½ inch. Turn under and press to seal. Scallop the edges by twisting between thumb and forefinger.

In the center of the top crust, insert a knife and cut out a rectangle about 7 x 3 inches; cut into the corners with a slash about ½ inch. Scallop the edges of the inside of crust in the same way as before. Dip a pastry brush into beaten egg and brush the top of the crust (this will glaze crust with a golden sheen when baked). Bake at 425° for 30 minutes or until the crust is golden brown.
Yield: 8 servings.

Creamed Sweetbreads

This is no longer served at the boarding house, but with early boarders it was a delicacy and a favored dish.

1 pound sweetbreads
1 cup white sauce, heated
1 teaspoon salt
1 teaspoon dried red pepper flakes
1 tablespoon parsley, chopped

Boil the sweetbreads; drain and remove the skins or membrane. Season the white sauce with salt, red pepper flakes, and parsley flakes and pour it over the sweetbreads. Spoon over toast and serve.
Yield: 6 servings.

Supper Liver and Potato Dumplings

3 tablespoons butter
12 chicken livers, cooked and chopped
2 cups dry mashed potatoes
1 cup bread crumbs
2 tablespoons onion, minced
1 tablespoon parsley, minced
2 eggs
Salt and pepper to taste

In a skillet melt the butter and cook the chicken livers until just done. Drain and chop the livers. In a bowl combine the livers with the remaining ingredients. Shape into balls about 1½ inches in diameter. Drop into boiling salted water and cook for 7 to 10 minutes.
Yield: 6 servings.

Mary Lou's Salmon Cakes

1 16-ounce can red Sockeye salmon, drained and flaked
¾ cup oatmeal
⅓ cup milk
1 egg, slightly beaten
3 tablespoons onion, finely minced
3 tablespoons green pepper, chopped
Oil

In mixing bowl, combine the salmon, oatmeal, milk, egg, and vegetables. Stir to blend. Shape into six patties, pressing firmly to hold together. In a large skillet heat oil and pan fry by browning on both sides. Excellent with tartar sauce, white sauce with cheese added, or with ketchup.
Yield: 6 servings.

Salmon Loaf

1 8-ounce package noodles
1½ cups cream style cottage cheese
1 cup sour cream
1 small onion, finely chopped
1 clove garlic, minced
2 teaspoons Worcestershire sauce
½ teaspoon salt
1 16-ounce can red Sockeye salmon, drained
½ cup sharp Cheddar cheese, shredded
1 cup potato chips, crumbled

In a large saucepan cook the noodles per package directions and drain. Combine the drained noodles, cottage cheese, sour cream, onion, garlic, Worcestershire, salt, and salmon; stir to blend. Grease a 2-quart loaf pan and spoon mixture into the pan. Layer the top with shredded cheese and potato chip crumbs. Bake at 325° for 40 minutes.
Yield: 6 to 8 servings.

Christmas Dinner for Family and Friends

Miss Mary hosts a table of friends and family for Christmas dinner, circa 1967. Holidays for Miss Mary were special times to invite close friends in the community to join her and her family for a *festive meal. A time to laugh, catch up on the local news, and enjoy each other. Hospitality is as much a hallmark of Miss Mary's as is the excellent food.*

Lynchburg

Lynchburg is a town-square town with the courthouse smack in the middle. Small shops with awnings and boardwalks—now replaced by paved sidewalks—have surrounded the square since the early days. The Farmers Bank has been on the north side of the square since it was chartered in 1888. The Lynchburg Hardware and General Store occupies part of the building where Mr. Jack Daniel owned and operated the White Rabbit Saloon at the turn of the century. The drugstore, the grocery, the farmers co-op, the auto store, and the Moore County News are part of the conglomerate of businesses on the square. A town park with a bandstand gazebo is directly across from the old Moore County Jail, which is now a museum.

One-half block off the square to the south sits the large white Greek Revival-style home known since 1908 as the Bobo Hotel. During World War II, the name was changed to Miss Mary Bobo's Boarding House.

One block north and across the footbridge over Mulberry Creek is the Jack Daniel Distillery.

These two businesses have made Lynchburg famous.

Southern Fried Catfish

½ cup cornmeal
¼ cup all-purpose flour
2 eggs
1 cup milk
6 to 10 catfish fillets (or 4 whole catfish,
  skinned)
Salt and pepper to taste
Vegetable oil for frying

In a shallow bowl mix the cornmeal and flour together. In a separate bowl beat the eggs and milk together. Salt and pepper the fish. Soak the fish in the milk mixture for 10 to 15 minutes. Drain well. Roll the fish in the cornmeal mixture. Heat the oil in a heavy skillet to 375° (should be very hot). Add the fish, being careful not to overcrowd. Turn as each side browns. Remove from the oil and drain. Leftover oil may be used to fry hush-puppies for added flavor.

Yield: 4 servings.

Moore County Oyster Casserole

2 tablespoons butter
1½ tablespoons all-purpose flour
1 cup milk (or half-and-half)
Salt and pepper
2½ cups cracker crumbs
1 pint shucked oysters with juice
¼ cup butter

In a saucepan melt the butter over low heat. Stir in the flour. Slowly add the milk and stir until thickened. Season with salt and pepper. Grease a 1½-quart casserole dish and sprinkle 1 cup of cracker crumbs on the bottom of the dish. Cover with half of the oysters, then half of the sauce. Repeat the layers with 1 cup of crumbs, the remaining oysters, and sauce. Sprinkle with the remaining crumbs. Dot with butter. Bake at 350° for 15 to 20 minutes, or until brown and bubbly.
Yield: 4 to 6 servings.

Stuffed Peppers

6 large bell peppers
1½ teaspoons salt
1 pound ground chuck
1 small onion, peeled and finely chopped
1 cup cooked rice
1 15-ounce can tomato sauce
1 tablespoon Worcestershire sauce
Ketchup

Cut top from each bell pepper, seed and core. In a large stew pan cover peppers with water and add ½ teaspoon salt. Bring to boil and boil for 5 minutes. Remove peppers from water, drain and place in shallow baking dish.

Combine the ground chuck, onion, remaining salt, rice, tomato sauce, and Worcestershire sauce, blend well. Lightly stuff each pepper with about ½ cup of the meat mixture. Place upright in baking dish. Top each pepper with splash of ketchup, cover dish and bake at 350° for 45 minutes. Remove cover and bake 15 minutes longer.
Yield: 6 servings.

Cabbage Pot Supper

1 pound ground round steak
1 large onion, chopped
*1 large cabbage head (about 2 lbs.), coarsely
    chopped*
Salt and pepper to taste
1 cup chicken broth
¼ cup Soy sauce

In a large skillet brown the ground steak, breaking it up with fork tines. Add the onion and let it brown slightly. Add cabbage. Sprinkle salt and pepper over all. Carefully add the chicken broth to skillet and pour Soy sauce over all; cover and simmer until the cabbage is tender, about 15 minutes.

Note: This was always served with a potato dish. Even simple boiled new potatoes in their jackets, salted and buttered, are good.
Yield: 8 servings.

Sunday One-Dish Breakfast

12 thick slices bread with crusts removed
½ cup butter
½ pound fresh mushrooms, sliced
2 cups onions, thinly sliced
Salt and pepper to taste
1½ pound pork sausage
1 pound Cheddar cheese, grated
5 eggs
2½ cups milk
2 tablespoons Dijon mustard
Parsley for garnish

Line the bottom of a well-greased 13 x 9-inch baking dish with the bread slices, overlapping as necessary. In a large skillet melt the butter and sauté the mushrooms and onions until tender. Season with the salt and pepper and set aside.

In a large skillet fry the sausage, breaking with fork into small chunks as it cooks. When brown, drain the excess fat. Over the bread in the baking dish layer half each of sausage, onion mixture, and cheese. Repeat the layers. In a bowl beat together the eggs, milk, and mustard. Pour the mixture over the layers. Cover and refrigerate overnight. Starting in a cold oven bake at 350°, uncovered, for 50 to 60 minutes, or until set. Serve garnished with parsley.
Yield: 8 servings.

Creole Scrambled Eggs

½ pound bacon
1 dozen eggs, beaten
1 4-ounce can chopped green chilies, drained
1 4-ounce jar diced pimiento, drained
¼ cup butter
1 bunch green onions, chopped
1 fresh tomato, peeled and diced
1½ cups fresh mushrooms, diced

In a heavy skillet cook the bacon until crisp; drain, crumble, and set aside.

In a large bowl combine the eggs, chilies, and pimiento. In a large, clean skillet, melt the butter and sauté the onion, tomato, and mushrooms until tender. Add the egg mixture. Cook over medium heat, stirring often, until the eggs are firm but still moist. Spoon onto serving platter and garnish with bacon crumbles. Serve immediately.
Yield: 6 servings.

Cooks Preparing for Mid-Day Dinner

Louise Gregory, here making pies, was mentioned in Miss Mary's memoirs for being a good cook. Certainly her pies and pastries have tempted guests to indulge more than they meant to at the table.

During the summer, fresh tomatoes and peppers are picked each morning to be prepared for the mid-day dinner.

Saturday's Saucy Eggs

½ cup butter
1 pound onions, peeled and sliced
6 tablespoons flour
2 cups chicken broth
Salt and pepper
1 cup cream
2 egg yolks, beaten
8 hard-boiled eggs
2 cups hot cooked rice

In a large skillet melt the butter and sauté onion over medium heat for about 10 minutes, stirring constantly and being careful not to brown. Sprinkle the flour over the onions and continue to cook for a couple of minutes, then add the chicken broth and season generously. Reduce heat and simmer for 15 minutes. In a small bowl combine the cream and beaten egg yolks, then carefully pour into onion mixture. Cut the hard-boiled eggs in half lengthwise and gently place into the sauce. Allow to heat thoroughly, but do not cook. Spoon over hot cooked rice and serve! Voila! A dinner fit for a King!
Yield: 4 to 6 servings.

Country Ham Casserole

Sauce

3 tablespoons butter
3 tablespoons flour
2 cups milk

In a saucepan over medium heat melt butter, but do not brown. Slowly add half of the milk. In a cup stir flour into remaining cup of cold milk to dissolve flour. Stir into warm milk and cook, stirring constantly, until sauce is thickened. Set aside.

¾ cup butter cracker crumbs (such as Ritz)
4 eggs, hard-boiled, peeled, and chopped
1 cup Cheddar cheese, grated
2 cups country ham, ground or finely chopped

In a casserole dish sprinkle half the crumbs, then half the eggs, half the cheese; ¼ sauce, half the ham, ¼ sauce. Repeat, finishing with crumbs. Bake at 350° for 30 minutes.
Yield: 6 to 8 servings.

Side Dishes

Southern Fried Okra

1½ cups sliced fresh okra, blanched and cooled
    (or 1 10-ounce box frozen sliced okra)
1 cup cornmeal
½ cup all-purpose flour
½ teaspoon salt
Pepper to taste (optional)
Vegetable oil (or lard)

If using frozen okra, allow it to thaw. Place the okra in a colander to drain for 30 minutes before proceeding. In a shallow bowl mix cornmeal, flour, and salt. Add pepper if desired. Roll the okra in cornmeal to coat each piece, then set aside for 1 hour. This will keep the coating from falling off during the frying.

In a large skillet (or deep-fat fryer) heat ½ inch of oil or more. When the oil is hot add the okra pieces 1 layer deep and cook until brown, about 5 minutes. Roll with a fork to turn and brown on the other side. Remove the cooked okra to a paper towel to drain.

Cover with a paper towel to keep warm while cooking the remaining okra. Remove to a warm oven prior to serving, if needed.

Note: Do not crowd frying okra: leave enough space to keep slices turning so as not to burn. At the boarding house an iron skillet is used for frying okra.
Yield: 6 servings.

Miss Mary's Cabbage Casserole

½ small head cabbage, chopped
1 small onion, chopped
½ bell pepper, chopped
Salt to taste
3 tablespoons butter
3 tablespoons all-purpose flour
1 cup milk
½ cup Cheddar cheese, shredded
Seasoned cornbread crumbs

In a saucepan cook the cabbage, onion, and bell pepper in lightly salted water until tender. Drain. In a saucepan melt the butter. Stir in the flour and cook for 1 minute, stirring constantly. Add the milk slowly and stir until thickened. Add the cheese and blend until melted. Remove the pan from the heat.

In a buttered 1½-quart casserole dish layer the drained vegetables and cheese sauce. Make several layers, ending with the sauce on top. Bake at 325° until bubbly. Top with seasoned crumbs. Return to the oven until lightly browned. We use cornbread crumbs that are sprinkled with poultry seasoning, but you could use packaged stuffing mix.
Yield: 4 servings.

Harvard Beets

2 tablespoons butter
1 tablespoon cornstarch
3 tablespoons sugar
¼ teaspoon salt
⅓ cup vinegar
2 cups small whole beets, cooked (or drained
   canned beets)

In a saucepan melt the butter and add the cornstarch, sugar, and salt. Blend in the vinegar. Heat, stirring constantly, until thick. Add the beets and heat thoroughly.
Yield: 4 to 6 servings.

Sweet Cabbage

2 tablespoons bacon drippings (or shortening)
1 pound cabbage, chopped
1 large onion, chopped
3 large apples, peeled, cored, and chopped
½ cup seedless raisins
3 tablespoons cider vinegar
1 tablespoon sugar
3 tablespoons apple jelly (or whatever flavor
   you have)
Salt and pepper

In a large skillet heat bacon drippings. Add the cabbage and onion and stir to coat. Lower the heat and cover to simmer for about 10 minutes. Add the remaining ingredients with one-half cup water, cover and simmer for about 45 minutes, stirring once or twice to blend. Add a small amount of water if needed.
Yield: 6 to 8 servings.

Celery Casserole

1 cup buttered bread crumbs
4 cups celery, chopped
1 cup Cheddar cheese, grated
½ cup slivered almonds
2 cans cream of celery soup

Spread bread crumbs on a baking sheet and place under the broiler to lightly brown. Preheat oven to 325°.
   In a buttered 1½-quart baking dish, spread a little over half of the bread crumbs. Layer with celery, cheese, and almonds; spoon one can of celery soup over top; repeat, reserving small amount of cheese and a few almonds for the top of casserole with the remaining bread crumbs. Bake at 325° for one hour.
Yield: 8 servings.

Green Rice Casserole

1½ cups uncooked instant rice
1 pint sour cream
1 10½-ounce can cream of celery soup
2 4-ounce cans chopped green chilies,
   undrained
Salt to taste
1 cup sharp Cheddar cheese, shredded
1 cup American cheese, shredded

Cook rice according to directions on box. In a mixing bowl combine the cooked rice, sour cream, soup, chilies, and salt. Stir to blend. In a lightly buttered 13 x 9-inch baking dish pour half of the rice mixture. Combine the cheeses and sprinkle half the cheese over the rice. Repeat the layers. Cover. Bake at 350° for 50 minutes.
Yield: 8 servings.

Sweet Onion Casserole

1 cup uncooked long-grain rice
6 large sweet onions
½ cup butter
¼ teaspoon salt
¼ teaspoon white pepper
1 cup Swiss cheese, shredded
1 cup half-and-half
Paprika

Cook the rice according to directions. Meanwhile, peel and chop the onions. In a large skillet over medium heat melt the butter. Add the onion and cook for 15 minutes, stirring frequently to keep from browning. Remove the pan from the heat and stir in the cooked rice, salt, pepper, cheese, and half-and-half. Pour into a lightly buttered 13 x 9-inch baking dish. Cover with foil. Bake at 350° for 30 minutes. Sprinkle with paprika and serve.
Yield: 10 to 12 servings.

Fresh Corn Casserole

8 ears sweet yellow corn
3 eggs
2 cups half-and-half, divided
2 tablespoons sugar
½ teaspoon salt
½ teaspoon dried red pepper flakes (optional)
¼ cup butter, melted

Shuck the corn, removing all silks. Wash and then with a sharp knife carefully cut the kernels off, slicing close to the cob. Then with the edge of the knife carefully scrape the cob to release all the milk from the remaining kernels.

In a separate bowl beat the eggs until light and golden. Add the corn to the eggs. Add 1 cup of the half-and-half, sugar, salt, and red pepper flakes, if desired. Transfer the corn mixture to a buttered baking dish and pour the remaining half-and-half and melted butter over the top. Bake at 350° for 35 minutes. Remove from the oven and let casserole sit for 5 minutes before serving.
Yield: 8 to 10 servings.

Miss Mary's Famous Baked Apricot Casserole

1 17-ounce can apricot halves, drained
1 cup light brown sugar, firmly packed
1½ cups butter cracker crumbs (Ritz or Town House crackers)
½ cup butter

In a greased casserole dish arrange the apricot halves cut side up. Sprinkle first the brown sugar and then the cracker crumbs over the apricots. Dot the crumbs with butter. Bake at 350° for 35 minutes, or until the casserole has thickened and is crusty on the top. Yum!
Yield: 4 to 6 servings.

Mr. Tom's Bedroom

This bedroom was Mr. Tom Motlow's during his later years. A bachelor, he lived at the boarding house for more than forty years. President of the Farmers Bank of Lynchburg from 1916 to 1967, Mr. Tom was held in high esteem by everyone who knew him. During the depression, when the federal government closed all banks, it is said that Mr. Tom did business out of the bank's back door to accommodate his neighbors. Consequently, the people of Lynchburg were able to stay afloat while the rest of the country felt their ships were sinking. Tom Motlow was the younger brother of Lem Motlow, who inherited the distillery from their uncle, Jack Daniel.

Spanish Rice

4 tablespoons butter
1 cup long-grain white rice, uncooked
1 teaspoon salt
1 teaspoon chili pepper
2½ cups water
1 rib celery, chopped
5 medium fresh tomatoes, peeled and chopped
   (or 16-ounce can diced tomatoes)
l large onion, chopped
1 bell pepper, diced
½ teaspoon dried red pepper flakes
1 tablespoon bacon drippings (optional)

In a large skillet that has a lid melt the butter. Add the rice, salt, and chili pepper and stir to blend. Cook over high heat until very lightly brown, stirring constantly to keep from burning. Add 2½ cups of water and bring the mixture to a boil. Lower the heat, cover, and allow the rice to cook for about 10 minutes.

Add the remaining ingredients. Continue to simmer for 15 to 20 minutes. Add extra liquid if needed, so the rice will be thick and moist, not dry.

Note: If using fresh tomatoes and there is minimal liquid, you may need to add more water, ½ cup at a time. Bacon drippings were traditionally added for flavor. Omit for those watching their fat intake.

Yield: 6 to 8 servings.

Southern Greens and Pot Likker

1 ham hock (or 4 strips bacon, or 2 ounces
   diced salt pork)
2 cups water
1 pound turnip greens (or mustard greens, or
   collard greens)
½ teaspoon dried red pepper flakes
3 hard-boiled eggs, sliced or quartered

In a large pan combine the ham hocks and water. Bring the water to a boil. Cover, reduce the heat, and simmer for 2 hours, adding water as needed to maintain 2 cups. (If using bacon or salt pork, fry in heavy saucepan until crisp. Remove the bacon or salt pork from the drippings. Add water to the rendered fat.)

While the ham hocks cook, wash the greens, removing the stems and discarding any limp, wilted, or blemished leaves. Tear into pieces.

Skim the fat from the ham hock liquid. Remove the hocks and cut meat into small pieces. Discard the skin and bones. Return the meat to the liquid and add the dried red pepper flakes. Place the greens in the pan (as the greens wilt, press them down and add more until all the greens are in the pan). Cover and simmer over low heat for 25 to 35 minutes. Greens may be served drained with the pot likker served in a gravy boat on the table, or serve the greens in the pot likker.

Garnish the greens with sliced or quartered hard-boiled eggs. Pepper sauce or a vinegar cruet should be placed on the table. Pot likker is excellent spooned over cornbread.

Yield: 8 to 10 servings.

Garden Carrot Casserole

2 pounds carrots, scraped and cut into rounds
3 tablespoons butter
1 large onion, chopped
¼ cup all-purpose flour
2 cups milk
1½ cups sharp Cheddar cheese, shredded
1 teaspoon dry mustard
½ teaspoon celery salt
Cracker crumbs
Butter

In a saucepan cook the carrots in lightly salted water until tender. Drain. In a skillet melt the butter and sauté the onion until tender. Stir in the flour and slowly add the milk. Cook over medium heat, stirring constantly, until thickened. Add the cheese, mustard, and celery salt. Stir until the cheese is melted. In a buttered casserole dish layer the carrots with the cheese sauce. Top with cracker crumbs. Dot with butter. Bake at 325° for 20 to 25 minutes, or until lightly browned and bubbly.
Yield: 6 to 8 servings.

Cauliflower with Cheese Sauce

1 large head cauliflower, separated into florets
½ teaspoon salt
3 tablespoons butter
3 tablespoons all-purpose flour
1 cup milk
¼ teaspoon salt
¼ teaspoon white pepper
½ cup aged sharp Cheddar cheese, grated
Paprika

In a saucepan cook the cauliflower in water with ½ teaspoon of salt. Cook for 5 minutes, until tender. Drain in a colander.

In a medium saucepan melt the butter over low heat. Stir in the flour to blend, and slowly add the milk. Cook, stirring constantly until the sauce thickens. Add salt, pepper, and cheese, and gently stir until melted. Place the hot cauliflower in a deep bowl. Pour hot cheese sauce over the cauliflower and sprinkle with paprika to garnish. Serve immediately.
Yield: 6 servings.

Tipsy Sweet Potatoes

4 large sweet potatoes
¼ cup butter, softened
¾ cup sugar
⅛ teaspoon salt
¼ cup Jack Daniel's Whiskey
½ cup broken pecans, lightly toasted

In a large pan cook the unpeeled sweet potatoes in just enough water to cover completely. Bring to a boil, cover, and cook until tender, about 35 minutes. Drain and cool, then peel off the skins. In a mixing bowl mash the potatoes with the butter. Add the sugar, salt, and Jack Daniel's Whiskey.

In a buttered 1½-quart round casserole dish, spread half of the potatoes and sprinkle with half of the pecans. Repeat the layers. Bake at 325° until hot, about 30 minutes.

Note: Light brown sugar may be substituted for white sugar to give a different (caramel) taste to this dish.
Yield: 6 to 8 servings.

MOUSE WAS GENERALLY the major domo during this period. He lived in the tenant house in back of the boarding house. The tenant house had rooms for two servants.

Eady was a black lady who cooked for the house during this period of time, and she lived in the other room in the tenant house. Eady always wore long calico dresses, an apron over her dress, and a ruffled dust cap on her head. After Eady finished her work, she would sit in her doorway and smoke a corncob pipe. Joan was a little girl, and she loved to sit beside Eady in the doorway. Sometimes Eady would talk to Joan, but at other times Eady would talk to herself and Joan would simply listen to her mumble.

Mary Lou Whittaker began cooking at the house after Eady's death. She reputedly made the best pastry in the world. Mary Lou cooked at the house for more than twenty years before her poor health forced her to quit.

When Cliffe and Jack were small there was a cook named Millie. Millie was a very large black lady with a sense of humor. She would put flour all over her face and young Jack would be so frightened that he would run from the kitchen.

Lucy was a black lady who came to do the washing in the basement hall, and she had a very large black washpot out back. As a small girl, Joan loved to watch Lucy as she rubbed the clothes on a washboard and churned around the pot while boiling the clothes.

Macaroni and Cheese

8 cups water
2 teaspoons salt
¼ cup vegetable oil
2 cups macaroni
2½ cups grated American cheese, divided
¼ cup butter

In a large saucepan bring the water and salt to a boil. Add the oil and macaroni, stirring occasionally. Cook until tender; drain. Add 2 cups of the grated cheese and butter. Pour the mixture into a buttered 13 x 9-inch baking dish. Top with the remaining cheese. Bake at 350° for 30 minutes, or until hot and bubbly.
Yield: 6 to 8 servings.

Vi's Famous Baked Tomatoes

3 cups canned tomatoes, drained and chopped
1 cup sugar
1 cup butter
1 teaspoon basil
6 slices toasted white bread, crumbled

In a saucepan heat the tomatoes, sugar, and butter until the butter melts. Add the basil and bread crumbs and continue simmering for about 15 minutes, until most of the liquid is absorbed. Pour into a greased 9-inch baking dish. Bake at 350° for about 20 minutes, or until thick.
Yield: 6 servings.

Cheese Pudding

12 slices stale bread, cubed
1 pound Cheddar cheese, grated
3 cups milk
4 eggs, well beaten
1 teaspoon dry mustard
1 teaspoon salt
⅓ cup butter, cut into pieces

Spread the bread cubes onto a baking sheet and place in oven to lightly brown. Butter a 1½-quart baking dish. Spread the bread cubes into the dish. In a medium bowl combine cheese, milk, eggs, dry mustard, and salt; pour over bread cubes. Place butter pieces on top of the mixture. Refrigerate for two hours or up to overnight. Bake at 300° for one hour.
Yield: 12 servings.

Upside-Down Sweet Potatoes

No need to wait until the holidays for this treat!

3 pounds sweet potatoes
¼ cup butter
½ cup sugar
1 teaspoon vanilla
1 teaspoon cinnamon
1 cup marshmallows
1 cup coconut flakes

Bake potatoes in their skins, peel and place in a medium mixing bowl. Mash with butter, sugar, vanilla, and cinnamon. Stir to blend well. Butter a 1½-quart baking dish. Line the bottom and up the sides with the marshmallows, then sprinkle with coconut. Spoon potatoes over coconut.

Topping
¼ cup butter
½ cup brown sugar
½ cup pecan pieces

In a small saucepan melt butter and stir in brown sugar. Sprinkle pecans over the top of potatoes and pour sugar mixture over all.

Bake at 350° for 10 to 15 minutes, until hot and bubbly.
Yield: 8 to 10 servings.

Hoppin' John's Black-eyed Peas

1 pound dried black-eyed peas
Water
½ pound hog jowl
1 large onion, chopped
½ teaspoon dried red pepper flakes
1 cup long-grain rice, cooked as directed on
* package*
Salt and pepper to taste

In a saucepan cover the peas with water. Bring to boil and then turn off the heat. Let the peas sit overnight, or at least 1½ hours.

Drain and return to the pan. Cover the peas with 6 cups of water and add the hog jowl, onion, and red pepper flakes. Bring to a rolling boil, reduce the heat, and simmer, adding water as needed. Stir in the cooked rice and season to taste. Simmer until the peas are thick to stir. This is excellent with Hot Water Hoe Cakes (see page 65).
Yield: 8 to 10 servings.

Louise and Ervin Crutcher's Egg Nog Party

Louise Crutcher, Miss Mary's daughter, was a wonderful cook. She loved to entertain in her home, and she did so beautifully. She belonged to three bridge clubs and often entertained the club members. Louise and Ervin Crutchers' egg nog party was an annual Christmas event that their many friends looked forward to with great anticipation. Ervin made the egg nog, and Louise prepared a table of goodies. This photo taken at their party was used on a Jack Daniel's calendar for December 1973. Miss Mary is noticeably absent, as she did not drink. Louise also served boiled custard for their family's Christmas dinner and would always have a small silver pitcher filled with Jack Daniel's on the table to be passed for those wanting to add it to the boiled custard.

Pineapple Casserole

½ cup butter, softened
¾ cup sugar
4 eggs
1 20-ounce can crushed pineapple
1 teaspoon lemon juice
¼ teaspoon nutmeg
3 cups stale white bread, cubed

In a medium mixing bowl cream butter and sugar and add eggs and beat well to blend. Add pineapple and carefully stir to blend, add lemon juice and nutmeg. Fold in bread cubes. Spoon into a buttered 1½-quart baking dish and bake at 350° about 45 minutes—until top is lightly golden.
Yield: 6 to 8 servings.

Yankee Limas

1 pound dried lima beans
1 teaspoon salt
½ cup maple syrup
¼ cup butter
4 strips of bacon

In a large saucepan cook beans as directed on package. Simmer with the salt until tender. Drain and reserve liquid. Place in a 2-quart baking dish. Combine the reserved liquid, syrup, and the butter, blend well. Pour over the beans. Place bacon strips over the top of the beans and bake covered at 325°, for 1½ hours. Remove cover and continue to bake for 30 minutes.
Yield: 8 servings.

Breakfast Potatoes

6 potatoes, peeled and grated
1 medium onion, peeled and grated
2 large eggs, slightly beaten
½ cup flour
Salt and pepper
Oil

In a large bowl combine the potatoes, onion, eggs, and flour. In a large skillet heat oil. Spoon the potato mixture into the hot oil, salt and pepper the top generously. Reduce heat to medium, brown on both sides, remove to platter and serve hot. May sprinkle with paprika, if desired.
Yield: 8 servings.

Cornmeal Soufflé

2 cups milk
¾ cup cornmeal
1 teaspoon salt
2 tablespoons bacon drippings (or butter)
3 eggs, separated

In the top of a double boiler, place milk and heat until hot (do not boil). Add cornmeal to hot milk while stirring constantly. Cook until it resembles a stiff sauce. Remove to cool, stir in salt and bacon drippings. In a small bowl beat egg whites until very stiff. In another bowl, lightly beat the egg yolks; add yolks to meal mixture, stiring to blend well. Fold in the egg whites. Spoon into a soufflé dish that has been well buttered. Bake at 350° for 25 minutes. Remove from oven and serve at once.
Yield: 6 to 8 servings.

Summer Corn Pie

5 slices bacon
1½ cups cornbread, crumbled
2 medium tomatoes, sliced
1 bell pepper, chopped
1 teaspoon salt
1 teaspoon sugar
2 tablespoons butter
4 ears fresh corn, husked, silked, kernels cut
  and cob scraped
2 cups sharp Cheddar cheese, grated

In an 8-inch square baking dish arrange the bacon slices on the bottom and curving up the sides. Sprinkle over the bacon 1 cup of the cornbread crumbs. Next layer half of each of the ingredients as follows: tomato slices, bell pepper, salt, sugar, butter, and corn. Repeat with another cup of cornbread crumbs and the layers. Top with the grated cheese and remaining cornbread crumbs. Bake at 350° for 25 minutes. The pie will be hot, bubbly, and lightly browned.
Yield: 8 servings.

Creole Grits

2 cups quick-cooking grits
2 quarts boiling water
2 teaspoons salt
½ cup butter, melted
10 slices bacon
1 large onion, chopped
1 cup celery, finely chopped
1 small bell pepper, chopped fine
1½ cups canned diced tomatoes, undrained
Freshly ground pepper
3 dashes hot sauce (optional)

In a large saucepan cook the grits in boiling salted water according to the package directions. Remove the pan from the heat and stir in the melted butter. In a skillet fry the bacon. Remove and drain on a paper towel, reserving the drippings. Using the same skillet sauté the onion, celery, and bell pepper in the bacon drippings.

Chop the bacon. In a large bowl stir the bacon pieces, onion, celery, pepper, and tomatoes into the grits. Add a dash of freshly ground pepper and hot sauce, if desired. Serve hot.

Note: This is a delicious accompaniment to southern catfish. Leftovers are delicious — just store in the refrigerator and reheat with a small amount of liquid or reheat in the microwave.
Yield: 10 to 12 servings.

Country-Style Green Beans

2 pounds fresh green beans
5 slices bacon, cut into small pieces
1 teaspoon salt
½ teaspoon dried red pepper flakes
½ teaspoon sugar
1⅓ cups water

Trim the beans and break them into about 1-inch pieces. In a saucepan combine the beans and the remaining ingredients. Simmer covered for about 60 minutes.
Yield: 8 servings.

Dining Room Conversation

(L-R) The boarding house major-domo; Ted Simmons, Jack Daniel's advertising copywriter for all these many years; Roger Brashears, who heads the visitor center at the distillery; and Ervin Crutcher, Miss Mary's son-in-law, who lived next door.

Roger Brashears lived at the boarding house from 1967 to 1973. He paid $60.00 per month for a room with a private bath and three meals a day. When Jack and Mary Bobo opened the boarding house in 1908, they charged $13.50 per month with two to a room and no private bath.

Photo courtesy of Joan Crutcher Ferguson

Old-Fashioned Pickled Beans

2 pounds freshly picked string, snap, or wax
  beans (or 1 pound freshly hulled pink beans,
  or 1 pound pinto or dried white beans,
  cooked)
5 cups apple cider vinegar
¾ cup sugar
1 teaspoon salt

If you are using dried beans, cook as usual,
just until tender. Fresh beans should be
cooked to the tender but firm stage. Place the
beans in a glass dish with a cover.

In a large pan combine the vinegar, sugar,
and salt and bring to the boiling point. Pour
the vinegar mixture over the beans and stir
to mix. Cover the dish and allow the flavors
to meld at least 2 hours before serving. May
be served either hot or cold.
Yield: 6 to 8 servings.

Stewed Okra and Tomatoes

4 cups fresh okra, small 2½-inch size
3 tablespoons bacon drippings (or butter)
1 large onion, chopped
4 fresh tomatoes (or 1 16-ounce can stewed
  tomatoes)
½ teaspoon salt
Salt and pepper to taste

Wash the okra (do not cut off the stem end
so the okra will not cook up slick or gooey).
Place in colander to drain. In a large
saucepan heat the bacon drippings and sauté
the onion until translucent. Add the okra,
tomatoes, salt, and just enough water to
cover, and simmer for about 30 minutes.
Adjust the taste with salt and pepper and
serve hot.
Yield: 6 to 8 servings.

Sideboard Potatoes

6 medium potatoes
1 teaspoon salt
2 large onions, peeled and sliced
1 cup celery, minced
2 cups half-and-half
2 cups Cheddar cheese, shredded
¼ cup butter

Peel and slice the potatoes. In a large saucepan parboil the potatoes in lightly salted
water to partially cook. In a greased shallow
baking dish, arrange the potatoes and onion
slices so they slightly overlap each other.
Sprinkle with salt and pepper. Spread
minced celery over top. Pour half-and-half
over all, top with shredded cheese, and dot
with butter. Cover and bake at 350° for 45
minutes. Uncover and continue baking for
15 minutes.
Yield: 6 to 8 servings.

Garlic Cheese Grits Casserole

4 cups water
1 teaspoon garlic powder (or more to taste)
1 teaspoon salt
¼ teaspoon pepper
1 cup quick-cooking grits
2 tablespoons butter or margarine
1½ cups grated processed cheese, divided
4 eggs, beaten
½ cup milk

In a large saucepan bring the water to a boil. Add the garlic powder, salt, and pepper. Gradually stir in the grits. Lower the heat and simmer, stirring occasionally, for 5 minutes. Remove the pan from the heat and stir in the butter and 1 cup of cheese until melted. In a small bowl mix the eggs with the milk. Stir the mixture into the grits. Pour the grits into a greased 2-quart casserole dish. Sprinkle with the remaining cheese. Bake at 350° for 1 hour.
Yield: 6 servings.

Hominy Casserole

¼ cup butter
¼ cup all-purpose flour
1 teaspoon onion powder
2 cups milk, heated
1 cup processed cheese, grated
1 29-ounce can hominy, drained
1 cup Ritz cracker crumbs
¼ cup butter

In a large saucepan melt the butter over low heat. Blend in the flour and onion powder. Slowly stir in the milk. Stir the sauce with a wire whisk or wooden spoon over low heat until thickened and smooth. Stir in the cheese until melted. Add the hominy. Pour into a greased casserole dish. Sprinkle with cracker crumbs and drizzle with melted butter. Bake at 350° for 30 minutes, or until hot and bubbly.
Yield: 6 servings.

Summer Squash Casserole

2 tablespoons butter
¼ cup bell pepper, chopped
¼ cup onion, chopped
2 cups yellow squash, cut into pieces, cooked, and well drained
¼ cup chopped pimiento
1 10¼-ounce can cream of mushroom soup
1 egg, beaten
½ cup processed cheese, grated
Salt and pepper to taste
½ cup cornbread crumbs
2 tablespoons butter, melted
¼ teaspoon poultry seasoning

In a pan sauté the bell pepper and onion in butter. In a medium bowl combine the bell pepper and onion, squash, pimiento, soup, egg, cheese, salt, and pepper. Place the mixture in a greased 1½-quart casserole dish. In a small bowl combine the cornbread crumbs, butter, and poultry seasoning. Sprinkle the crumb mixture on top of the squash casserole. Bake at 350° for 30 minutes, or until bubbly.
Yield: 6 servings.

Miss Mary with Dill Dismukes just before dinner, June 23, 1977

From Miss Mary's memoirs: "A few years ago I started feeding the Jack Daniel Distillery's invited guests and am not open to the public any more. They fixed two dining rooms down in the basement, and we have the two upstairs. During the winter, we just use the upstairs but during the rest of the year, we feed from 50 to 100 people, five days a week. Dill Dismukes and Louise Gregory are the cooks, and they are good ones, too. I stay out of the kitchen now. But up until age 98, I still ordered the groceries, planned the menus, wrote the checks, etc. I wonder how many more business people kept going at that age!"

Photo courtesy of Joan Crutcher Ferguson

Pure Delight Turnips

3 pounds fresh white turnips, diced
Bacon drippings
¼ cup butter, melted
2 teaspoons sugar
1 teaspoon salt
¼ teaspoon pepper
3 eggs
1 teaspoon vinegar
1 cup bread crumbs
Paprika

In a saucepan cook the turnips in boiling salted water seasoned with bacon drippings until tender. Drain. In a large bowl combine the turnips, butter, sugar, salt, pepper, eggs, and vinegar. Blend in the bread crumbs. Spoon into a greased 2-quart casserole dish. Sprinkle with paprika. Bake at 375° for 40 to 45 minutes.
Yield: 8 servings.

Turnips with Ham Hock

2 ham hocks
8 medium sized turnips, peeled and sliced
2 medium white potatoes, peeled and sliced
1 teaspoon sugar
Salt and pepper to taste

In a large stew pot cover the ham hocks with water; boil until tender. Remove hocks to cool. Add turnips, potatoes, and sugar; bring to a boil. Boil until tender. Drain and mash, adjust seasonings. While turnips are cooking, remove meat from hocks. Discard bones and skin. Add pulled meat to mashed turnips and stir to blend.

Note: This can be served with bottled hot pepper sauce, if desired.
Yield: 8 to 10 servings.

Country-Fried Corn

Recipes in the South take advantage of the fresh produce readily available to them. The summer provides ample tomatoes, corn, onions, and many other fresh vegetables. This is a favorite dish in the South, using the sweet corn so abundant during the summer. Miss Mary's guests have enjoyed it for almost one hundred years!

6 ears fresh corn
3 slices country bacon (or pork side meat or, best of all, country ham fat)
⅔ cup water
2 tablespoons sugar
¼ cup milk
2 teaspoons cornstarch
1 tablespoon butter
Salt to taste

Use a sharp knife to cut the tips of kernels, then the remainder of the kernels, from ears of corn into a large bowl. Scrape the cobs with a knife to get out all of the liquid. Set the bowl aside. In a heavy skillet cook the bacon until crisp (if using side meat or ham fat, cook until the fat is rendered). Remove the bacon from the skillet, drain, crumble, and reserve. Stir the corn into the hot bacon drippings. Add water and sugar. Cook, stirring constantly, until the mixture begins to thicken. Gradually stir the milk into the cornstarch until smooth. Add the cornstarch mixture to the corn. Cook over low heat until thickened. Stir in the butter and salt. Serve topped with the crumbled bacon.
Yield: 6 servings.

Potato Pancakes

Bacon drippings (or vegetable oil)
2 cups potatoes, grated
2 tablespoons onion, grated
3 eggs, beaten
1½ teaspoons salt
1½ tablespoons all-purpose flour

In a heavy skillet heat the bacon drippings. In a medium bowl combine the remaining ingredients. When the skillet is hot, ladle about 2 to 3 tablespoons of mixture for each pancake into the drippings. Brown on one side, turn, and brown on the other. Serve hot with sour cream or with Mushroom Sauce (see page 88).

Note: These are delicious for breakfast with bacon and eggs.
Yield: 12 to 14 pancakes

Skillet Potatoes

½ cup butter, melted (or olive oil)
8 large potatoes, peeled and sliced ¼ inch thick
1 large onion, chopped
1 bell pepper, diced
Salt and pepper to taste
½ cup water
Paprika (optional)

In a large iron skillet melt the butter. Add a layer of sliced potatoes, onions, and bell pepper and season with salt and pepper. Repeat until all of the vegetables are in the skillet. Add water, cover, and cook over medium heat for 35 minutes. To serve, drain off any liquid or fat; turn out onto a platter and garnish with paprika, if desired.
Yield: 8 servings.

Glazed Carrots

8 carrots
¼ cup butter
2 tablespoons Jack Daniel's Whiskey
1 tablespoon brown sugar or honey

Peel the carrots and cut them in quarters lengthwise and then in half crosswise. In a skillet cook the carrots in salted water until tender-crisp, about 10 minutes. Do not overcook. Drain. Push the carrots to one side of the skillet and add the butter, Jack Daniel's Whiskey, and sugar, stirring to combine. Stir in the carrots over medium-high heat, shaking the skillet to coat the carrots. Cook until lightly brown. Serve immediately.
Yield: 4 servings.

Elegant Onions

8 onions, peeled and quartered
Salt and pepper to taste
2 cups saltine cracker crumbs
3 tablespoons butter
¾ cup half-and-half, room temperature
2 eggs, beaten
½ cup buttered bread crumbs

In a medium saucepan cover the onions with water. Add a pinch of salt and boil just until tender. Drain and place half the onions in shallow baking dish; sprinkle with salt, pepper, and a layer of cracker crumbs, repeat and dot with butter. Combine half-and-half and eggs, carefully pour over all, and top with buttered bread crumbs. Bake at 350° for 20 minutes or long enough to set eggs and lightly brown top.
Yield: 6 to 8 servings.

Tennessee Squash Casserole

3 tablespoons butter
½ small onion, finely chopped
1 cup hot milk
1 cup dry bread crumbs
Salt and freshly ground pepper to taste
¼ teaspoon nutmeg
2 eggs, slightly beaten
2 cups squash, cooked, drained, and mashed
½ cup pecans, chopped
¼ cup Jack Daniel's Whiskey

In a small skillet melt the butter and sauté the onion until tender. Add the milk and pour it over the bread crumbs. Stir to mix well. Season with salt, pepper, and nutmeg. Fold in the eggs, squash, pecans, and Jack Daniel's Whiskey. Pour into a 1½-quart greased baking dish. Bake at 325° for 30 minutes, or until set.
Yield: 4 servings.

Old-Time Stewed Potatoes

6 medium potatoes, peeled and thickly sliced
½ teaspoon salt
4 cups water
2 tablespoons all-purpose flour
Cold water
¼ cup butter
Salt and pepper to taste

In a large saucepan cook the potatoes in salted water until tender. Remove the pan from the heat. In a cup add enough cold water to the flour to make a thin paste. Stir well to remove all lumps. In a thin stream, slowly stir the paste into the potato water. Return the saucepan to the heat and simmer until slightly thickened. Add butter and adjust salt to taste. Freshly ground pepper may be used to garnish.
Yield: 6 servings.

Miz Crutcher's Convent Pudding

No one seems to know why this was so named, but it is certainly unusual. It was suggested that this came about during the deprivation and shortages during the Second World War, when many households served meatless dishes.

1 cup macaroni
2 cups milk, scalded
2 cups soft bread crumbs
½ cup butter
2 cups Cheddar cheese, grated
2 tablespoons bell pepper, minced
1 small onion, minced
3 eggs, slightly beaten
1 teaspoon salt

In a saucepan cook the macaroni until tender. Drain. In the saucepan or a large bowl combine the macaroni and the remaining ingredients and stir to blend. Pour into a greased 1½-quart casserole dish. Bake at 325° for 30 minutes. Serve with Mushroom Sauce (see page 88), if desired.
Yield: 6 to 8 servings.

A Vice-President (to be) Honors Miss Mary on Her 99th

Former state representative Albert Gore, Jr., talks with Louise Crutcher at Miss Mary's 99th birthday celebration. Some other notables who are known to have eaten at the boarding house: Frank James, Andrew Jackson, former Tennessee governors Bob Taylor, Lamar Alexander, and Ned Ray McWherter.

Also, Speaker of the House Sam Rayburn was said to have eaten here when he visited Tennessee, as have the Ambassador to Russia and various stars of stage and screen.

Photo courtesy of Joan Crutcher Ferguson

Our Best Baked Beans

6 slices bacon
1 large onion, chopped
1 medium green pepper, chopped
2 16-ounce cans pork and beans
¼ cup brown sugar, firmly packed
1 teaspoon Worcestershire sauce
1 teaspoon dry mustard
1 cup catsup
1 tablespoon molasses
¼ cup Jack Daniel's Whiskey

In a skillet cook the bacon until done but not yet crisp. Remove the bacon from the pan, drain, chop, and set aside.

Drain all but 2 tablespoons of drippings from the skillet. Add the onion and pepper and sauté until soft. In a 1-quart casserole combine all of the ingredients except the bacon. Top with the bacon. Bake at 350° for 40 to 45 minutes.
Yield: 8 servings.

Asparagus and Egg Casserole

24 fresh asparagus spears, cooked until tender
    (or 2 10-ounce packages frozen)
6 hard-boiled eggs, sliced
2 cups white sauce
1 cup sharp Cheddar cheese, grated
1 teaspoon lemon juice
1 tablespoon Worcestershire sauce
Salt to taste
Butter cracker crumbs

White Sauce

¼ cup butter
¼ cup all-purpose flour
2 cups half-and-half

Layer the asparagus and egg slices in a buttered 13 x 9-inch casserole dish. To the white sauce, add the cheese, lemon juice, Worcestershire sauce, and salt. Cook over medium heat, stirring constantly, until the cheese has melted. Pour sauce over the asparagus and eggs. Top with the cracker crumbs. Bake at 350° for 20 to 25 minutes, or until bubbly and browned.
Yield: 8 servings.

Cakes

Country Raisin Cake

1 cup seedless raisins
2½ cups water
6 tablespoons shortening
1 teaspoon baking soda
½ cup Jack Daniel's Whiskey
2 cups all-purpose flour
1 cup sugar
½ teaspoon salt
1 teaspoon cinnamon
1 teaspoon allspice
1 teaspoon cloves
1 teaspoon orange rind, finely grated
½ cup pecans, broken
Confectioners' sugar

In a small saucepan cook the raisins in water for 20 minutes. Drain, reserving ½ cup of the liquid. To the hot liquid add the shortening and baking soda, stirring to mix well. In a large bowl combine the shortening mixture, cooked raisins, and Jack Daniel's Whiskey. In a medium bowl sift the dry ingredients together and add the orange rind. Add this mixture to the batter along with the pecans. Mix well. Pour the batter into a greased and floured Bundt pan. Bake at 375° for 40 to 45 minutes. Cool slightly before removing. Sift confectioners' sugar over the top of the cake and cool.
Yield: 12 servings.

Chocolate Spirit Fruitcake

1 18¼-ounce package devil's food pudding cake mix
⅓ cup Jack Daniel's Whiskey
1 cup sour cream
3 eggs
2 cups chopped pecans
1 cup golden raisins
1 cup maraschino cherries, drained and halved
1 cup candied pineapple pieces, halved
1 6-ounce package semisweet chocolate chips
Corn syrup (optional)

In a large bowl combine the cake mix, Jack Daniel's Whiskey, sour cream, and eggs on low speed until moistened, then beat for 2 minutes on high speed. Stir in the remaining ingredients except the corn syrup. Pour the batter into a greased and floured 12-cup fluted tube pan. Bake at 350° for 50 to 60 minutes or until cake springs back when touched lightly in the center. Cool for 20 minutes. Turn out on a rack and cool completely. To serve, brush warm corn syrup on the top for a glossy finish. Slice thinly for serving. Cake will keep for two weeks wrapped tightly in foil or plastic and stored in the refrigerator.
Yield: 12 to 15 servings.

100th Birthday Celebration

Miss Mary with daughter Louise and son Charles, at her 100th birthday gathering at the boarding house. Her birthday was announced coast to coast by Willard Scott on NBC's "Today Show." Former Tennessee senator Albert Gore, Jr., sent greetings and a U.S. flag that had flown over the Capitol in Washington. She received a birthday card from then-president and Mrs. Ronald Reagan, and Lynchburg declared Mary Bobo Day in honor of the town's oldest living resident.

Photo courtesy of Joan Crutcher Ferguson

Italian Cream Cake

½ cup shortening
½ cup butter
2 cups sugar
5 eggs, separated
2 cups all-purpose flour
1 teaspoon baking soda
1 cup buttermilk
1½ cups coconut
1 teaspoon vanilla extract
1 cup walnuts, chopped

In a large bowl cream the shortening, butter, and sugar, beating until smooth. Add the egg yolks, beating well. In a separate bowl combine the flour and baking soda. Add the dry ingredients to the creamed mixture alternately with the buttermilk. Stir in the coconut, vanilla, and nuts. In a small bowl beat the egg whites until stiff. Fold them into the cake batter. Pour the batter into 3 greased 8-inch cake pans. Bake at 350° for 25 minutes, or until a cake tester inserted in the center comes out clean.

Frosting

1 8-ounce package cream cheese, softened
¼ cup butter, softened
1 16-ounce box confectioners' sugar
1 teaspoon vanilla extract
½ cup walnuts, chopped

In a medium bowl beat the cream cheese and butter until smooth. Add the confectioners' sugar and vanilla, beating until smooth. Ice the cake layers and sprinkle chopped nuts on top.
Yield: 12 servings.

Applesauce Cake

½ cup butter, softened
1 cup brown sugar
1 cup sugar
1 egg
2 cups applesauce
2 teaspoons baking soda
2½ cups all-purpose flour
2 teaspoons cinnamon
1 teaspoon cloves
½ teaspoon nutmeg
2 tablespoons cocoa
1 teaspoon salt
1 cup pecan pieces
1 cup raisins (optional)

In a large mixing bowl cream together the butter, brown sugar, sugar, and egg. In a smaller bowl combine the applesauce and baking soda. Add the applesauce mixture to the sugar mixture. In a separate bowl sift together the flour, spices, cocoa, and salt. Add the dry ingredients to the sugar mixture with an electric mixer on medium until blended. Stir in the pecans and raisins. Pour into a greased 13 x 9-inch pan (or 2 8-inch cake pans). Bake at 375° for 25 to 30 minutes, or until a cake tester inserted in the center comes out clean. Frost with your favorite chocolate or caramel frosting. It is also delicious served with Jack Daniel's Dessert Sauce (see page 182).
Yield: 15 servings.

Porch Sitting

An afternoon pause on the front porch of the boarding house. Miss Mary once said that she had seen Lynchburg grow from a tranquil town of about 400 residents to a thriving town of about 400 residents. "The biggest change in Lynchburg," she said, "is all the out-of-town folk that come through here."

Photo courtesy of Joan Crutcher Ferguson

Miss Mary Bobo's Boarding House Gingerbread with Lemon Sauce

1 cup molasses
½ cup sugar
½ cup butter, softened
½ cup boiling water
1 egg, beaten
3 cups all-purpose flour
½ teaspoon salt
1 teaspoon baking soda
1 teaspoon cinnamon
1 teaspoon ground ginger
½ teaspoon ground allspice

In a large pan combine the molasses and sugar with an electric mixer. Add the butter. Slowly add the boiling water, mixing well. Stir in the egg. In a separate bowl combine the dry ingredients. Add them to the molasses mixture. Pour the batter into a greased and floured 13 x 9-inch baking pan. Bake at 350° for 25 to 30 minutes or until the cake springs back when lightly touched in the center. Cool in the pan. To serve, cut into squares and top with Lemon Sauce.

Lemon Sauce

1 tablespoon cornstarch
½ cup sugar
Pinch of salt
1 cup boiling water
2 tablespoons lemon juice
1 teaspoon lemon rind, grated

In a small saucepan mix the cornstarch, sugar, and salt. Stir in the boiling water. Bring to a boil, stirring constantly, and cook until thickened. Remove the pan from the heat, add the lemon juice and rind, and mix well. Serve warm or cool.
Yield: 15 to 18 servings.

Pineapple Sheet Cake

2 cups sugar
2 cups all-purpose flour
½ cup vegetable oil
2 eggs
1 20-ounce can crushed pineapple with juice
1 teaspoon baking soda

In a medium bowl combine all of the ingredients. Pour into a well-greased 13 x 9-inch sheet cake pan. Bake at 350° for 20 minutes or until a cake tester inserted in the center comes out clean. (If using a 13 x 11-inch pan, bake a few minutes longer.) While the cake bakes, prepare the icing.

Icing

1 cup sugar
½ cup butter, softened
⅔ cup evaporated milk
Pinch of salt
½ cup pecans, chopped
½ cup coconut

In a saucepan combine the sugar, butter, milk, and salt. Bring to a boil and then lower the heat. Cook and stir for 10 minutes. Remove the pan from the heat. Add the pecans and coconut. Pour the icing over the hot cake and allow it to cool before cutting.
Yield: 15 to 20 servings.

Confederate Fruitcake

Everybody loves this one!

1 cup butter
2 cups sugar
2 eggs, slightly beaten
3½ cups all-purpose flour
1 teaspoon baking soda
¼ teaspoon salt
1 teaspoon cinnamon
¼ teaspoon nutmeg
¼ teaspoon cloves
1½ cups applesauce
¼ cup Jack Daniel's Whiskey
1 pound small gumdrops (if larger ones are
   used, cut into small pieces)
1 cup pecans, chopped
½ cup all-purpose flour

In a large bowl cream the butter and sugar until light and fluffy. Add the eggs and beat well. In a separate bowl combine 3½ cups of flour, the baking soda, salt, and spices and add the mixture alternately to the batter with the applesauce and Jack Daniel's Whiskey. In a small bowl combine the gumdrops, pecans, and the remaining flour. Gently stir them into the batter.

Pour the batter into a greased and floured 9-inch tube pan. Bake at 325° for 1 hour and 45 minutes, or until the cake tester comes out clean. Cool. This cake is moist and keeps well. It is excellent served with The Gentleman's Sauce flavored with Jack Daniel's Whiskey (see page 142).
Yield: 16 servings.

Orange Candy Cake

⅔ cup oil
1 16-ounce can pumpkin
2⅔ cups sugar
4 eggs
½ cup water
½ cup Jack Daniel's Whiskey
3 cups all-purpose flour
2 teaspoons baking soda
½ teaspoon baking powder
1 teaspoon salt
2 teaspoons cinnamon
½ teaspoon nutmeg
¼ teaspoon cloves
1½ cups orange slice candy, cut into small
   pieces
⅔ cup pecans, broken
⅓ cup all-purpose flour

In a large bowl combine and blend the oil, pumpkin, sugar, eggs, water, and Jack Daniel's Whiskey. In a separate bowl combine 3 cups of flour, baking soda, baking powder, salt, and spices. In a smaller bowl combine the candy pieces, pecans, and remaining flour. Add the liquid ingredients to the dry ingredients and mix well. Stir in the candy and pecans. Pour the batter into a greased and floured 10-inch tube pan. Bake at 350° for 1 hour to 1 hour and 10 minutes, or until done when tested with a cake tester. Cool inverted in the pan on a rack for 15 minutes, then remove from the pan.

Topping

1 8-ounce package cream cheese, room
   temperature
¼ cup Jack Daniel's Whiskey
1 8-ounce carton whipping cream
¼ cup sugar

In a bowl blend the cream cheese and the Jack Daniel's Whiskey with a mixer. In a separate bowl whip the cream, adding the sugar gradually. Beat until stiff. Gently fold the whipped cream into the cream cheese. Refrigerate until time to serve. Top each slice of cake with a dollop of cream and garnish with orange candy slices and crushed pecans, if desired.
Yield: 12 to 15 servings.

Cream Cake

This one's richer than Rockefeller!

½ *cup butter, softened*
3 *cups sugar*
6 *eggs*
1 *tablespoon lemon extract*
3 *cups sifted cake flour*
1 *cup whipping cream (do not whip)*

In a large bowl cream the butter and sugar until light and fluffy. While beating with a mixer, add the eggs one at a time. Add the extract, flour, and whipping cream as needed to keep the batter flowing until all is combined. Pour the batter into a well-greased and floured 9-inch tube or Bundt pan. Bake at 350° for 60 minutes, or until a cake tester inserted in the center comes out clean.

Note: This is excellent toasted for breakfast. It needs no icing but is excellent as a base for strawberry shortcake.
Yield: 10 to 12 servings.

Miss Mary's Pineapple Upside-Down Cake

1 16-ounce can pineapple slices, drained (or crushed pineapple)
½ cup butter, melted
1 to 1¼ cups brown sugar
3 eggs
2 cups sugar
2 cups all-purpose flour
2 teaspoons baking powder
1 cup milk
½ cup butter
2 teaspoons vanilla

In the bottom of a 13 x 9-inch cake pan arrange the pineapple slices. Drizzle ½ cup of melted butter over all, then sprinkle enough brown sugar to cover the bottom of the pan and absorb the melted butter. Set the pan aside.

In a large mixing bowl beat the eggs until light yellow. Add the sugar and beat well. In a separate bowl combine the flour and baking powder and add the mixture to the batter. In a small saucepan heat the milk and remaining butter over medium heat. Bring the milk to the boiling point, but do not allow it to boil. Gradually add the hot milk to the cake batter, beating to mix well. Add the vanilla and mix to blend. The batter will be thin. Gently pour the batter over the pineapple in the cake pan. Bake at 350° for 35 to 40 minutes, or until a cake tester inserted in the center comes out clean.

This can be turned out on a large platter to serve or cut into squares and served on dessert plates. Originally this was baked in a covered iron skillet on the top of the stove, but baking is more easily controlled in the oven for today's cooks.
Yield: 12 to 15 servings.

Four Generations

This photo was taken of Miss Mary, with daughter Louise, granddaughter Joan Crutcher Ferguson, and great-granddaughter Mary Ferguson on the day that the photographer took Miss Mary's picture for the famous Jack Daniel's ad that brought thousands of birthday cards, thirty-six birthday cakes, numerous gifts, and countless good wishes to Miss Mary on her 99th birthday. What did Miss Mary say about the ad? "Well, the distillery didn't put the ad in Playboy like they usually do, but if they had, I bet I would have been the only ninety-nine-year-old lady pictured there."

Hummingbird Cake

3 cups all-purpose flour
2 cups sugar
1 teaspoon salt
1 teaspoon baking soda
3 eggs, beaten
1½ cups vegetable oil
1½ teaspoons vanilla extract
1 8-ounce can crushed pineapple, undrained
1½ cups pecans, lightly toasted and chopped
2 cups bananas, mashed

In a large mixing bowl combine the dry ingredients. Add the eggs, vegetable oil, stirring until the dry ingredients are moistened. Do not beat. Stir in the vanilla, pineapple, 1 cup of pecans, and bananas. Spoon the batter into 3 well-greased and floured 9-inch cake pans. Bake at 350° for 25 to 30 minutes, or until a cake tester inserted in the center comes out clean. Cool in pans for 10 minutes; remove to racks and cool. Spread with frosting.

Cream Cheese Frosting

2 8-ounce packages cream cheese, softened
1 cup butter, softened
2 16-ounce packages confectioners' sugar, sifted
2 teaspoons vanilla extract
½ cup pecans, lightly toasted and chopped

In a bowl combine the cream cheese and butter, beating until smooth. Add the confectioners' sugar, beating until light and fluffy. Stir in the vanilla and pecans.
Yield: 10 to 12 servings.

The Queen's Cake

1 cup butter, softened
3 cups sugar
6 eggs, separated
1 8-ounce carton sour cream
3 cups all-purpose flour, sifted
Dash salt
¼ teaspoon baking soda
1 teaspoon lemon extract
1 teaspoon vanilla extract

In a large mixing bowl cream the butter and sugar until light and fluffy. Add the egg yolks and continue beating until thoroughly mixed. Add the sour cream and flour with an electric mixer on low. Add the salt, baking soda, and extracts. In a separate bowl beat the egg whites until stiff. Fold the egg whites into the batter. Spoon the batter into a greased and floured 10-inch tube pan. Bake at 325° for 1½ hours, or until a cake tester inserted in the center comes out clean.

Excellent topped with Ambrosia Cream, or may be served plain.

Ambrosia Cream

1 16-ounce can pineapple chunks, undrained
1 8-ounce jar maraschino cherries, chopped
    with juice
1 20-ounce can flaked coconut
2 cups miniature marshmallows
1 cup pecans, chopped
1 16-ounce carton sour cream

In a large mixing bowl stir together the fruit, coconut, marshmallows, and pecans. Fold in the sour cream and stir to blend. Cover and refrigerate for at least 2 hours. Serve over sliced Queen's Cake or angel food cake.
Yield: 12 servings.

Prune Cake

2 cups all-purpose flour
1½ cups sugar
1 teaspoon salt
1 teaspoon cinnamon
1 teaspoon allspice
1 teaspoon nutmeg
1 teaspoon cocoa
3 eggs, beaten
1 cup vegetable oil
1 cup buttermilk
1 teaspoon vanilla extract
1 cup stewed prunes, chopped

In a large bowl sift together the dry ingredients. In another large bowl beat together the eggs, oil, buttermilk, and vanilla. Add the dry ingredients and stir in the prunes. Pour the batter into a greased and floured 10-inch tube pan. Bake at 325° for 50 to 55 minutes, or until a cake tester inserted in the center comes out clean. Cool in the pan for 15 minutes before turning out on a rack to cool completely.

This cake is good without frosting, but it is also excellent with The Gentleman's Sauce (see page 142), or you may frost with your favorite cream cheese icing.
Yield: 12 servings.

Colada Cake

¾ cup butter, softened
1¾ cups sugar
3 cups all-purpose flour, sifted
1 tablespoon plus 1 teaspoon baking powder
1 teaspoon salt
1 teaspoon vanilla extract
½ cup milk
1 8-ounce can pineapple, undrained
4 egg whites, stiffly beaten
1 7-ounce can flaked coconut
1 cup light brown sugar
6 tablespoons cream
½ cup butter
¼ cup Jack Daniel's Whiskey

In a large bowl cream ¾ cup of butter and 1¾ cups of sugar until light and fluffy. In a separate bowl sift the dry ingredients together. Add the vanilla to the milk. Stir the milk and dry ingredients alternately into the butter mixture. Stir in the pineapple. Fold in the beaten egg whites and coconut. Pour into a greased 9 x 5-inch loaf pan and bake at 350° for 40 minutes. About 10 minutes before the cake is finished baking, combine in a saucepan the brown sugar, cream, remaining butter, and Jack Daniel's Whiskey. Bring to a boil, then simmer for 3 minutes. After the cake has cooked for 40 minutes, remove it from the oven and pour the sauce over the top. Return to the oven and let the sauce bubble over the top of the cake, about 5 minutes.
Yield: 8 servings.

Old-Time Buttermilk Pound Cake

1 cup shortening
3 cups sugar
5 eggs, separated
½ teaspoon baking soda
1 teaspoon water
1 cup buttermilk
3 cups all-purpose flour
½ teaspoon salt
1 tablespoon vanilla extract

In a large mixing bowl cream the shortening and sugar. Add the egg yolks and beat to combine. Dissolve the baking soda in 1 teaspoon of water and stir into the buttermilk. Combine the flour and salt and add alternately with the milk to creamed mixture, beating well. Beat in the vanilla. In a separate bowl beat the egg whites until stiff peaks form. Fold the egg whites into the batter. Transfer the batter to a greased and floured 10-inch tube pan. Bake at 325° for 60 minutes. Check with a cake tester to allow for differences in oven temperatures. Serve plain or with Jack Daniel's Dessert Sauce (see page 182).
Yield: 12 servings.

Miss Mary's Birthday

When Jack Daniel's ran this ad with Miss Mary's picture, friends of Jack Daniel's certainly responded. Miss Mary received more than 8,000 birthday cards. One town in Michigan sent a huge card with every citizen's signature.

Carrot Cake with Cream Cheese Frosting

1½ cups vegetable oil
1 cup sugar
½ cup brown sugar
4 eggs
2 cups all-purpose flour
2 teaspoons baking soda
2 teaspoons baking powder
2 teaspoons cinnamon
1 teaspoon salt
3 cups carrots, finely shredded
1 cup pecans, chopped
1 cup raisins (optional)

In a large bowl combine the oil and sugars, beating until well blended. Add the eggs one at a time, mixing well. In a separate bowl sift the dry ingredients together and add to the batter gradually, beating until smooth. Stir in the carrots, nuts, and raisins. Pour into a greased and floured 13 x 9-inch cake pan. Bake at 325° for 45 minutes, or until a cake tester inserted in the center comes out clean. Cool.

Frosting

1 8-ounce package cream cheese, softened
½ cup butter, softened
1 16-ounce box confectioners' sugar
2 teaspoons vanilla extract

In a bowl whip the cream cheese and butter together. Beat in the sugar gradually until smooth. Stir in the vanilla. Refrigerate to store.
Yield: 12 servings.

Fresh Apple Cake

2 cups apples, diced
1 cup sugar
1 egg, beaten
1 cup all-purpose flour, sifted
1½ teaspoons cinnamon
1 teaspoon baking soda
½ cup pecans, chopped

In a large bowl combine the apples with the sugar and let stand until the sugar is dissolved. Stir in the egg. Sift the dry ingredients together and stir them into the apple mixture along with the pecans. Pour into a greased and floured 8-inch square pan. Bake at 375° for 40 minutes. Remove the cake from the oven and immediately cover with sauce while it is still hot.

Sauce

½ cup light brown sugar, firmly packed
½ cup sugar
2 tablespoons all-purpose flour
1 cup water
¼ cup butter
1 teaspoon vanilla extract

In a saucepan mix the sugars with the flour. Add the water and cook over medium heat until thickened. Stir in the butter until melted. Remove the pan from the heat and stir in the vanilla. Pour over the cake.
Yield: 8 servings.

Miss Mary Turns 100

Miss Mary Bobo celebrates her 100th birthday with friends and family at the boarding house where she had lived for seventy-three years. She joined the Lynchburg Methodist Church when she was fifteen. At her birthday celebration, the minister said that Miss Mary, the oldest living member, was almost as old as the church.

Photo courtesy of Joan Crutcher Ferguson

Dried Fruitcake

1 cup golden raisins
1 apple, peeled and grated
1 cup walnuts, chopped
1 cup mixed dried fruits, chopped
1 tablespoon orange rind, grated
⅓ cup orange juice
⅓ cup Jack Daniel's Whiskey
1 teaspoon vanilla extract
3 cups all-purpose flour
1 teaspoon baking powder
½ teaspoon salt
1 cup butter
1½ cups sugar
4 eggs

In a bowl combine the raisins, apple, walnuts, dried fruit, and orange rind. Stir in the orange juice, Jack Daniel's Whiskey, and vanilla; let stand for 30 minutes while preparing the cake batter.

In a medium bowl sift together the flour, baking powder, and salt. Set the bowl aside. In a large mixing bowl cream the butter and sugar with an electric mixer until light and fluffy. Add the eggs one at a time, beating well after each addition. Gradually add the dry ingredients, blending until smooth. Fold in the fruit and nut mixture. Spoon the batter into a greased and floured 10-inch tube pan. Bake at 325° for 1½ hours to 1 hour and 40 minutes, or until a cake tester inserted in the center comes out clean. Cool in the pan for 10 minutes. Turn onto a wire rack and cool. Place the cake on aluminum foil and drizzle with 2 tablespoons of Jack Daniel's Whiskey. Bring the foil up and wrap securely. Store at room temperature to mellow. Every 2 or 3 days, unwrap and spoon 2 tablespoons of Jack Daniel's Whiskey over the top. The cake should mellow at least one week before serving.
Yield: 12 to 15 servings.

Spice Cake with Seafoam Frosting

⅓ cup butter
1 cup sugar
1 egg plus 1 egg yolk
2 tablespoons molasses
¾ cup milk
2¼ cups all-purpose flour
2 teaspoons baking powder
1 teaspoon cinnamon
¼ teaspoon ground cloves
½ teaspoon nutmeg

In a bowl cream the butter and sugar thoroughly until light and fluffy. Add the egg and yolk and continue to beat. Beat in the molasses and milk alternately with the dry ingredients. Grease and flour 2 8-inch or 2 9-inch cake pans. Spoon the batter into the pans. Bake at 375° for 25 minutes, or until a cake tester inserted in the center comes out clean. Remove the cake from the oven and cool on wire racks.

Seafoam Frosting

1½ cups brown sugar
½ cup water
¼ teaspoon cream of tartar
4 egg whites

In a saucepan boil brown sugar, water, and cream of tartar to make a syrup that will spin a thread. Remove the pan from the heat. With a mixer beat the egg whites until they foam up and start to hold their shape. While constantly beating, very slowly add the syrup. Frost the cooled cake.
Yield: 10 to 12 servings.

Fresh Coconut Cake

Nothing spells the South like fresh coconut cake. Traditionally this is made for Thanksgiving and Christmas dinners. In Tennessee two other cakes are served at those dinners, Jam Cake and Caramel Cake. These are the three that Miss Mary Bobo's Boarding House always serves for holiday dinners.

1 fresh coconut
1 cup butter
2 cups sugar
8 egg whites
1 teaspoon vanilla extract
¼ teaspoon almond extract
1 cup milk, divided
3¼ cups all-purpose flour
4 teaspoons baking powder
¼ teaspoon salt
¼ cup coconut milk
⅓ cup confectioners' sugar

Prepare the coconut as follows: Pierce three eyes with an ice pick. Drain and reserve the liquid. Bake the coconut at 400° for 15 minutes. This will cause the hard shell to crack open. Have a bowl ready to catch the coconut milk. Split the coconut in half (sometimes a hammer is useful) and pry the meat from the shell with the point of a sharp knife. Carefully cut the brown membrane off of the coconut with a knife or vegetable peeler. Grate the coconut by hand or use a food processor. Store in a zip-lock bag in the freezer if you prepare in advance. A coconut will yield about 3 cups of grated coconut.

In a large mixing bowl cream the butter and sugar. Beat in the egg whites, then the extracts. Add ½ cup of milk and beat well. In a separate bowl combine the flour, baking powder, and salt. Gradually add the dry ingredients to the creamed mixture along with the remaining milk. Spoon the batter into 2 greased and floured 9-inch layer cake pans. Bake at 350° for 40 minutes, or until a cake tester inserted in the center comes out clean. Remove to wire racks and cool. When the cakes are cool, carefully split each layer in half horizontally. Mix ¼ cup of coconut milk and ⅓ cup of confectioners' sugar and spoon over each of the layers.

Icing

2 cups sugar
2 tablespoons light corn syrup
⅔ cup water
2 egg whites
2 teaspoons vanilla extract
½ teaspoon almond extract

In a medium saucepan bring the sugar, corn syrup, and water to a boil, stirring to dissolve the sugar. Cover the pan and allow the syrup to come to a full rolling boil. Remove the pan from the heat.

In a mixing bowl beat the egg whites until stiff. Carefully add ⅓ cup of the hot syrup in a thin stream while beating the egg whites. Return the pan to the heat and continue boiling without stirring until the temperature reaches 240° on a candy thermometer. With the mixer on high speed, gradually add the hot syrup to the egg whites. Add the extracts and continue beating until the icing is of spreading consistency, about 5 minutes longer.

To ice the cake, spread a small amount of icing on each layer and sprinkle with coconut. Repeat. The top layer should have sufficient icing for the top. Ice the sides and sprinkle with the remaining coconut. Let the cake sit for at least 10 minutes before cutting.
Yield: 20 to 24 servings.

Jam Cake with Cloud Icing

1 cup butter
2 cups sugar
1 teaspoon baking soda
1 cup buttermilk
4 egg yolks, lightly beaten
3 cups all-purpose flour
2 teaspoons cinnamon
1 teaspoon ground nutmeg
1 teaspoon ground allspice
1 teaspoon vanilla extract
1 cup blackberry jam
4 egg whites

In a large bowl cream the butter and gradually add the sugar. In a small bowl dissolve the baking soda in the buttermilk and add the egg yolks. In a separate bowl mix the flour and spices. Alternately add the buttermilk mixture and the dry ingredients to the creamed mixture. After the batter is thoroughly mixed, add the vanilla extract and the blackberry jam. In a small mixing bowl beat the egg whites until stiff, but not dry. Fold them into the batter. Spoon the batter into a greased and floured 10-inch tube pan. Bake at 300° for 15 minutes, then increase the oven temperature to 350° for 15 minutes. Increase again to 360° for 30 minutes. A cake tester inserted in the center should come out clean.

Cloud Icing

Jam Cake may be iced with the following for those who like iced cake.

2 cups sugar
1 cup water
3 egg whites

In a small saucepan boil the sugar and water to the soft-ball stage. Remove the pan from the heat.

In a small mixing bowl beat the egg whites with an electric mixer on high speed until stiff. Slowly add the sugar syrup and whip until it reaches spreading consistency. Ice Jam Cake.
Yield: 15 to 20 servings.

Dump Cake

1 20-ounce can crushed pineapple, undrained
1 cup light brown sugar
1 cup shredded coconut
1 cup pecans, chopped
1 18-ounce box yellow cake mix
½ cup butter, cut up
Whipped cream

Heavily spray a 13 x 9-inch baking pan with cooking spray. Set it aside.

Dump the crushed pineapple into the baking pan, carefully spreading to cover the bottom. Crumble ½ cup brown sugar over the pineapple. Sprinkle it with the coconut, pecans, and remaining sugar. Gently spoon the cake mix to cover, and pat down lightly. Dot with butter. Bake at 350° for 35 to 40 minutes. Cool. Cut into squares and top with whipped cream to serve.
Yield: 15 servings.

Miss Mary Bobo on her 101st birthday

The Tennessee Whiskey Cake

Tennessee is called the Volunteer State. This cake never fails to bring the Volunteers to fill their plates and test the recipe!

2 cups all-purpose flour
½ teaspoon nutmeg
6 eggs, separated
1 cup butter, softened
2 cups sugar
½ cup Jack Daniel's Whiskey
2½ cups raisins
1½ cups pecans, chopped

Place the flour in a dry skillet. Cook over medium heat while stirring until it is pale brown in color. This will make the cake a darker color and will add a slightly nutty flavor to the cake. Stir in the nutmeg and set it aside.

In a small bowl beat the egg whites until stiff. Set the bowl aside. In a large mixing bowl cream the butter and sugar until light and fluffy. Add the egg yolks and beat well. Add the Jack Daniel's Whiskey and stir to blend. Beat the flour into the creamed ingredients. Fold in the egg whites, raisins, and pecans. Pour the batter into a greased and floured 9-inch tube pan. Bake at 300° for 2½ hours, or until a cake tester inserted in the center comes out clean. Let the cake cool. You may refrigerate the cake before serving. Serve with ice cream or whipped cream, if desired.
Yield: 10 to 12 servings.

Tennessee Toddy Cake

1½ cups light brown sugar, firmly packed
1 cup sugar
1 cup butter, softened
6 eggs, separated
4 cups cake flour, divided
4 teaspoons baking powder
½ teaspoon allspice
½ teaspoon nutmeg
½ teaspoon cinnamon
⅔ cup Jack Daniel's Whiskey
½ cup molasses
2½ cups golden raisins
1 cup dried apricots, chopped
1 cup dates, chopped
3 cups pecans, chopped

In a large bowl beat the sugars and butter with an electric mixer until light and fluffy. Beat in the egg yolks. In a separate bowl combine 3 cups of flour, the baking powder, and spices. In a small bowl combine the Jack Daniel's Whiskey and molasses. Add the flour mixture to the batter alternately with the whiskey mixture. Mix the remaining flour with the fruit and nuts. Fold them into the batter. Beat the remaining egg whites until stiff but not dry. Fold them into the batter. Pour into 2 tube pans that have been greased and lined with wax paper. Bake at 325° for 1 hour, or until a cake tester inserted in the center comes out clean. Cool on a wire rack for 3 minutes before removing from the pans.
Yield: 24 to 30 servings.

The Gentleman's Sauce

1 cup sugar
1 tablespoon cornstarch
¼ teaspoon salt
1 tablespoon butter
1 cup boiling water
¼ cup Jack Daniel's Whiskey

In a small bowl combine the sugar, cornstarch, salt, and butter. Gently stir into the boiling water and cook until clear, about 5 minutes. Remove from the heat and stir in the Jack Daniel's Whiskey. Delicious spooned over cake, ice cream, or pudding.
Yield: 8 servings.

Pies

Heavenly Fudge Pie

3 ounces semisweet chocolate, chopped
2 ounces unsweetened chocolate, chopped
¼ cup butter
3 large eggs
1 cup sugar
1 cup dark corn syrup
2 teaspoons vanilla extract
1½ cups pecans, chopped
1 9-inch pie crust (pre-baked for 12 minutes only)

In the top of a double boiler over simmering water melt the semisweet and unsweetened chocolate pieces along with the butter, stirring often. Remove the pan from the water. In a large mixing bowl beat the eggs, sugar, and corn syrup, blending well. Carefully beat in the warm chocolate. Add the vanilla, blending well. Gently stir in the pecan pieces. Pour the filling into the prepared crust. Bake at 400° for 5 minutes. Reduce the temperature to 350° and bake for 30 minutes. The pie will puff up in the center. Remove the pan from the oven and cool for 1 hour before serving. Top with whipped cream.
Yield: 10 servings.

Our Favorite Apple Pie

The apples cook in their own juice without thickener.

Pastry for 2-crust 9-inch pie
⅔ cup sugar
⅛ teaspoon salt
¾ teaspoon cinnamon
6 apples, peeled, cored, and sliced
Butter
1 tablespoon sugar

Roll out half of the pastry to ⅛-inch thickness. Line a 9-inch pie plate and prick with a fork several times. Combine ⅔ cup of sugar, salt, and cinnamon. Place the apples in the pie shell and sprinkle the sugar mixture over all. Dot with ample butter. Roll out the remaining pastry and place it over the top of the apple filling. Moisten the edges to seal and press with fork tines. Slits should be cut in the top crust to allow steam to escape. Sprinkle the remaining tablespoon of sugar over the top crust. Bake at 425° for 50 minutes, until the top is brown and the apples are tender.

This pie is good as is, or you may serve it with ice cream, whipped cream, or cream.
Yield: 6 to 8 servings.

Guest Book

Miss Mary's guest book has signatures of guests from around the world, including such famous names as country music's Minnie Pearl, Tommy Overstreet, and Randy Travis; authors Alex Haley and Janet Dailey; and newspaper columnists Rex Reed and Liz Smith.

Photo by Hope Powell

Fallen Angel Pie

Diets fall by the wayside when this pie is served, but there will be no weeping, only shouts of praise!

3 egg whites, room temperature
Dash salt
1 teaspoon vanilla extract
1 cup sugar
¾ cup soda cracker crumbs
½ teaspoon baking powder
½ cup pecans, chopped

In a mixing bowl with an electric mixer on high speed, beat the egg whites until foamy. Add the salt and vanilla. Gradually beat in the sugar, a small amount at a time, until shiny and stiff. In a separate bowl combine the cracker crumbs, baking powder, and pecans. Fold the crumb mixture into the egg whites. Spoon in a greased 9- or 10-inch pie plate. Indent in center, spooning up on sides to shape like a crust. Bake at 325° for 30 to 35 minutes, until lightly browned. Remove and cool. Meanwhile, prepare topping.

Jack Daniel's Praline Topping

2 cups sugar
1 teaspoon baking soda
1 cup buttermilk
⅛ teaspoon salt
2 tablespoons butter
2 cups chopped pecans
⅓ cup Jack Daniel's Whiskey
1 teaspoon vanilla extract
1 quart vanilla ice cream, slightly softened

In a heavy saucepan combine the sugar, soda, buttermilk, and salt. Using a candy thermometer, cook until the mixture reaches 210°, stirring constantly. Add the butter and pecans and continue cooking and stirring until the thermometer reaches 235°. Remove the pan from the heat; stir in the Jack Daniel's Whiskey and vanilla. Beat by hand for a few minutes; it should be thick and gooey, not sugary.

Spoon slightly softened vanilla ice cream into the crust, smoothing the top. Cut into slices and top with the Jack Daniel's Praline Topping. Sit back and listen to the raves!
Yield: 8 servings.

Osgood Pie

2 cups sugar
½ cup butter, melted
½ cup pecans, chopped
1 cup dates, chopped
4 eggs, beaten
2½ tablespoons vinegar
1 teaspoon vanilla extract
1 teaspoon cinnamon
½ teaspoon allspice
1 unbaked 9-inch pie shell

In a medium bowl combine all of the ingredients except the pastry shell and blend well. Place the pastry shell in a 9-inch pie plate. Add the filling. Bake at 350° until the pie is set, about 30 minutes. Cool. Serve topped with a dollop of whipped cream.
Yield: 8 servings.

Jack Daniel's Pecan Pie

A favorite with guests and Lynchburg natives.

3 extra-large eggs, slightly beaten
1 cup sugar
2 tablespoons butter, melted
1 cup dark corn syrup
1 teaspoon vanilla extract
¼ cup Jack Daniel's Whiskey
½ cup semisweet chocolate chips
1 cup pecan halves
1 unbaked 10-inch pie shell

In a medium bowl combine the eggs, sugar, butter, syrup, vanilla, and Jack Daniel's Whiskey. Mix well. Sprinkle the chocolate chips over the bottom of the unbaked pie shell and add the pecans. Pour the filling over the chips and pecans. Bake at 375° for 35 to 40 minutes, or until a knife inserted about halfway between the center and the edge comes out clean. Set aside to cool.
Yield: 6 to 8 servings.

Old-Fashioned Egg Custard Pie

1 unbaked 9-inch pie shell
4 eggs
½ cup sugar
½ teaspoon salt
1 teaspoon vanilla extract
2 cups milk, scalded
Nutmeg

Partially bake the crust at 400° for 5 to 8 minutes. Remove from the oven and mash the bubbles in the crust down with the back of a spoon.

In a bowl combine the eggs, sugar, salt, and vanilla. Gradually stir in the scalded milk. Pour the filling into the pie shell. Sprinkle with grated nutmeg. Bake at 400° for 15 minutes. Reduce the oven temperature to 350° and continue baking for 15 to 20 minutes or until a knife inserted in the center comes out clean. Cool before serving.
Yield: 6 to 8 servings.

Yellow-Mallow Pie

1 Prepared Graham Cracker Crust
3 cups miniature marshmallows
1 20-ounce can crushed pineapple, drain and reserve syrup
1 cup whipping cream
1 teaspoon vanilla
¼ teaspoon salt

In a medium saucepan over low heat stir marshmallows and one-half cup of reserved syrup constantly until marshmallows are melted. Chill until thickened.

In a chilled bowl, beat the whipping cream until stiff. Fold in the marshmallow mixture until well blended. Add all but one-half cup of pineapple, along with the vanilla and salt. Pour into the prepared crust and garnish top with reserved pineapple. Chill for 2 hours before serving.
Yield: 6 to 8 servings.

A Visit to the White House and a Booksigning

Food is a wonderful introduction to many delightful people, and with the publication of two earlier cookbooks, we had occasion to meet some distinguished chefs. Publication of The Spirit of Tennessee Cookbook *got us an invitation to tour the White House kitchen. Here, along with Chef Anne Rosenzweig of Arcadia in New York, we had the opportunity to see the chefs prepare their first meal for President and Mrs. George Bush, who had just moved into the White House. Southern foods were being prepared for a luncheon for sixteen people that day. With the publication of* Hometown Celebration Cookbook *in 1990, the Fancy Food Show invited us to San Diego to autograph books for attendees. We shared the autograph table with well-known author and chef Paul Prudhomme.*

Photos by Doris Lynch

Guests Gather on the Lawn before Dinner

The big porch and shady lawn serve as the reception area for the guests as they arrive at the boarding house for dinner. The time is relaxed as guests park their cars in the driveway or stroll down the street from shopping on the square just a half block away. It is a chance to get into the sync of a time past, when mid-day dinner was a gathering from the little shops around the square and the distillery, a welcomed respite from the day's business. The dinner bell still calls the guests to the table, and as names are called from the reservation list, they follow their hostess to the dining room.

Lemon Meringue Pie

1½ cups sugar
¼ cup plus 1 teaspoon cornstarch
3 tablespoons all-purpose flour
¼ teaspoon salt
4 egg yolks
1½ cup water
⅓ cup lemon juice
¼ teaspoon lemon rind, grated
3 tablespoons butter
1 baked 9-inch pie shell

In the top of a double boiler over simmering water combine the sugar, cornstarch, flour, and salt. Beat the egg yolks with a fork until lemon colored and add to the sugar mixture along with the water. Cook, stirring constantly, until the mixture starts to thicken. Add the lemon juice and rind and cook for 5 minutes longer. Remove the pan from the heat and add the butter, stirring until melted. Allow the filling to cool before pouring into the cooled pastry shell.

Meringue

4 egg whites
8 tablespoons sugar
1 teaspoon vanilla extract

In a bowl beat the egg whites until stiff but not dry. Add the sugar gradually and then add the vanilla. Spoon the meringue over the cooled pie filling, pushing with the spoon to seal the edges with the pastry. Bake at 350° for 12 to 15 minutes, until lightly browned.
Yield: 6 to 8 servings.

Buttermilk Pie

1½ cups sugar
¼ cup butter
3½ tablespoons all-purpose flour
3 large eggs, beaten
½ cup buttermilk
½ teaspoon vanilla extract
1 unbaked 9-inch pie shell

In a medium bowl cream the sugar and butter. Add the flour, eggs, buttermilk, and vanilla. Pour the filling into the unbaked pie shell. Bake at 450° for 10 minutes. Reduce the temperature to 350° and bake for 30 minutes, or until set.
Yield: 6 to 8 servings.

French Coconut Pies

3 eggs
2 cups sugar
¼ cup butter, melted
1 teaspoon vanilla extract
3 tablespoons all-purpose flour
Pinch salt
1 cup half-and-half
2 cups coconut
2 unbaked 8-inch pie shells

In a large mixing bowl combine all of the ingredients except the shells, adding one at a time until the coconut has been mixed in. Stir until well blended. Pour the filling into the unbaked pie shells. Bake at 350° for 40 minutes. The center of the pies will be firm. Cool before cutting.
Yield: 12 servings.

Southern Coconut Pie

6 tablespoons butter, melted
1¼ cups sugar
1½ tablespoons all-purpose flour
3 large eggs
½ teaspoon vanilla
½ cup buttermilk
1 cup coconut
1 unbaked 9-inch pie shell

In a large mixing bowl combine the butter, sugar, and flour. Add the eggs and mix well. Add the vanilla and buttermilk and mix to blend. Stir in the coconut. Pour the filling into the pie shell. Bake at 350° for 35 to 40 minutes, until the filling is set and a light golden brown.
Yield: 6 to 8 servings.

Cumberland Mountain Chocolate Pie

1½ cups sugar
¼ cup cocoa
¼ cup butter, melted
2 eggs, beaten
1 5-ounce can evaporated milk
1 teaspoon vanilla extract
1 unbaked 9-inch pie shell

In a medium mixing bowl combine the sugar and cocoa. With the mixer on low add the butter, eggs, milk, and vanilla, blending well. Pour the filling into an unbaked pie shell. Bake at 350° for 30 to 40 minutes. The pie is done if the center is firm when gently shaken. To serve, top with a large spoonful of Custard Sauce Topping (see page 182).
Yield: 6 to 8 servings.

Rich Chocolate Meringue Pie

1 cup sugar
3 heaping tablespoons all-purpose flour
3 heaping tablespoons cocoa
3 large egg yolks
1½ cups whole milk
1 teaspoon vanilla extract
Baked 9-inch pie shell

In a saucepan combine the dry ingredients, stirring to remove any lumps in the cocoa. In a small bowl beat the egg yolks and add to the dry ingredients. Add the milk gradually and place over medium heat, stirring constantly to assure that the filling doesn't burn. Cook until thickened, then remove from heat and add the vanilla. Stir well, then pour into the baked pie shell.

Meringue

3 egg whites
2 tablespoons ice water
½ teaspoon cream of tartar
6 tablespoons sugar

In a mixing bowl combine the egg whites, ice water, and cream of tartar. Beat at high speed until the whites peak. Gradually beat in the sugar. Spoon the meringue over the pie filling, pushing with the back of the spoon to the crust edge. Bake at 475° for 5 minutes, until golden brown. Watch while the meringue browns so it will not brown too much.
Yield: 6 to 8 servings.

Mary Lou's Chess Pie

½ cup butter, melted
1½ cups sugar
¼ cup milk
3 eggs
1½ teaspoons vanilla extract
1 unbaked 9-inch pie shell

In a medium mixing bowl combine the melted butter, sugar, and milk. Add the eggs one at a time, using an electric mixer to blend well. Add the vanilla. Pour into the pie shell. Bake at 350° for 35 minutes. The center will be firm.
Yield: 6 to 8 servings.

Jeff Davis Pie

1 cup sugar
2 tablespoons all-purpose flour
¼ cup butter
Pinch salt
4 eggs
1 cup half-and-half
½ teaspoon ground nutmeg
1 teaspoon lemon extract
Unbaked 9-inch pie shell

In a medium bowl combine the sugar, flour, butter, and salt. Beat with a mixer to blend. Add the eggs, beating well. With the mixer on low add the half-and-half, nutmeg, and lemon extract. Pour the filling into the pie shell. Bake at 425° for 15 minutes (best if you place this on the lower shelf of the oven). Reduce the oven temperature to 350° and bake for 30 minutes, or until a knife inserted in the center comes out clean. Cool and serve.
Yield: 6 to 8 servings.

Boarding House Sour Cream Raisin Pie

1 cup sugar
2½ tablespoons all-purpose flour
1 teaspoon cinnamon
¼ teaspoon cloves
½ cup seedless raisins
½ cup pecans
1½ cups sour cream
3 large egg yolks, beaten
1 baked 9-inch pie shell
3 egg whites
6 tablespoons sugar

In the top of a double boiler combine the sugar, flour, and spices. Stir to blend. Add the raisins, nuts, and sour cream, and stir to combine. Place the double boiler over boiling water and bring the mixture to a boil. Add a small amount of the boiling filling mixture to the egg yolks, then slowly add the yolks to the filling, stirring constantly so the filling will not lump. Cook until thick. Remove the top pan from the heat and allow to cool. Pour into a baked pie shell. Beat the egg whites until they form stiff but not dry peaks, adding sugar gradually as you beat. Top the pie with the meringue and brown in a 300° oven. Remove and cool.
Yield: 6 to 8 servings.

Nature's Bounty

*Two gardens behind the boarding house produce
fresh vegetables, which during the growing season
are picked at the peak of the harvest and prepared
for mid-day dinner.*

Photos by Hope Powell and Pat Mitchamore

Easy Lovin' Sugar Pie

¼ cup Jack Daniel's Whiskey
¼ cup plus 1 tablespoon sugar
⅓ cup all-purpose flour
¾ cup brown sugar, firmly packed
1 unbaked 9-inch pie shell
2 cups half-and-half
1 teaspoon vanilla extract
1 teaspoon lemon juice
¼ cup butter, divided
Nutmeg

Prior to mixing the pie, in a small mixing bowl pour the Jack Daniel's Whiskey over the sugar. After sugar has absorbed the whiskey, proceed, reserving 1 tablespoon of the flavored sugar for final serving.

To the remaining sugar mixture add the flour and brown sugar. Sprinkle the mixture over the pie crust. Combine the half-and-half, vanilla, and lemon juice and carefully pour over the sugar mixture in the pie shell. Dot the top with butter pieces and then sprinkle with nutmeg. Bake at 350° for 40 to 45 minutes, or until set.

When the pie has cooled slightly, sprinkle the remaining flavored sugar over the top and serve.
Yield: 6 to 8 servings.

Our Never-Fail Meringue

8 tablespoons sugar
1 tablespoon cornstarch
¾ cup water
3 egg whites

In a small saucepan combine the sugar, cornstarch, and water. Cook over medium heat until it becomes a clear syrup and the sugar has completely dissolved.

In a small mixing bowl beat the egg whites until foamy. While continuing to beat the egg whites with the mixer on high, begin pouring in the hot syrup in a thin stream. Beat until the mixture stands in shiny peaks. Spread the meringue over the pie filling, carefully covering the filling to the edge of the crust. Bake at 475° until golden brown, about 5 minutes. Remove from the oven and cool.
Yield: meringue for one pie.

Caramel Pie

½ pound light caramels (about 28)
½ cup water
¼ cup butter
¾ cup sugar
¼ teaspoon salt
1 teaspoon vanilla extract
2 eggs, slightly beaten
1 cup nut pieces (pecans or walnuts)
1 unbaked 9-inch pie shell
Whipped cream (optional)

In the top of a double boiler over simmering water place the caramels, water, and butter. Cook and stir until the caramels melt and become a smooth sauce. In a mixing bowl combine the sugar, salt, vanilla, and beaten eggs. Stir to mix well. Stir in the caramel mixture and add the nuts, mixing well. Pour the mixture into the pie shell. Bake at 400° for 10 minutes. Reduce the heat to 350° and bake for 20 minutes. Remove and cool. To serve top with whipped cream, if desired.
Yield: 6 to 8 servings.

Breakfast for Celebrities

One special morning each October, Miss Mary Bobo's serves up a big Tennessee breakfast in honor of celebrities who come to judge the annual World Championship Barbecue. Waiting on the lawn for the bell are Pulitzer Prize-winning author Jory Sherman, columnist Rex Reed, actresses Colin Wilcox and Betty Lynn (better known as Thelma Lou from Mayberry), recording artist Tommy Overstreet, and a variety of sports and television personalities.

Bird's Fried Pies

1 8-ounce package dried apricots (or peaches)
2½ cups water, divided
1 cup sugar
3 cups all-purpose flour
½ teaspoon salt
½ teaspoon baking soda
½ cup shortening (or lard)
Buttermilk
Lard (or shortening) for frying

In a saucepan over high heat cover the dried fruit with 2 cups of water and bring to boil. Cook until the fruit begins to get tender and the liquid is reduced by ½ cup. Add ½ cup of water and 1 cup of sugar and continue to boil until the fruit is soft, thick, and mushy. Do not let the fruit burn. Stir occasionally. Set filling aside to cool.

In a large mixing bowl combine the flour, salt, and baking soda. Cut in ½ cup of shortening. Add enough buttermilk to make a dough. On a floured bread board roll the pastry out thinly. Cut in 5-inch rounds and place a spoonful of filling in the center of each round. Moisten the edges, fold over, and seal with fork tines.

In an iron skillet melt lard to about ½ inch deep. Gently place the pastries in the hot fat and fry until brown on one side. Do not overcrowd. Turn to brown the other side. Remove the pies from the pan and drain on paper towels. Sprinkle with sugar. Delicious hot or cold.
Yield: 8 pies.

Chocolate Pudding Pie

3¼ cups milk
1 cup sugar, divided
¼ cup butter
6 tablespoons cocoa
5 tablespoons cornstarch
½ teaspoon salt
1 teaspoon vanilla extract
3 large egg yolks, lightly beaten
1 baked 9-inch pie crust
1 8-ounce carton whipping cream

In a saucepan scald the milk with ½ cup of sugar and the butter. Set aside to cool.

In a medium mixing bowl combine ¼ cup of sugar, the cocoa, cornstarch, and salt. To this add some of the cooled milk, then the vanilla, stirring constantly. Return all of the cocoa mixture to the saucepan and cook over low heat, stirring constantly, until the mixture is smooth and thickened and comes just to a boil. Stir some of the hot cocoa mixture into the beaten egg yolks, then return the yolk mixture to the saucepan. Cook, stirring constantly, for about 2 minutes. Pour the filling into the baked pie crust. Bake at 300° for 55 minutes. Remove and cool on a wire rack, then cover and refrigerate.

To serve, whip the cream with the remaining ¼ cup of sugar until stiff peaks form. Spread on the pie, slice, and serve.
Yield: 6 to 8 servings.

Deep-Dish Peach Pie

Pastry for 1 double-crust deep-dish pie
4 cups sliced peaches (firm, ripe fruit)
½ cup sugar
1 cup brown sugar, firmly packed
2 tablespoons all-purpose flour
¼ cup butter, divided
½ cup water
¼ cup Jack Daniel's Whiskey
2 thin slices lemon with rind
1 teaspoon sugar

Line a deep pie dish with thinly rolled pastry. Place the peach slices over the pastry. In a small saucepan mix ½ cup of sugar, the brown sugar, flour, 2 tablespoons of butter, and water. Stir constantly until the mixture boils. Pour over the peaches. Sprinkle Jack Daniel's Whiskey over all, dot with the remaining butter, and top with the thin slices of lemon. Cover with the remaining pastry and sprinkle with 1 teaspoon of sugar. Bake at 350° for 40 to 45 minutes, until the fruit is bubbling and the crust is browned.
Yield: 8 servings.

Yesteryear's Lemon Pie

1 cup wet bread (see directions)
1 cup sugar
3 egg yolks, beaten
Juice of one lemon
¼ cup butter
Baked 8-inch pie shell
3 egg whites
3 tablespoons sugar

Dip the bread into a bowl of water until wet clear through. Remove and squeeze the water from the bread. Place the bread in a measuring cup. In the top of a double boiler combine the wet bread, 1 cup of sugar, egg yolks, lemon juice, and butter and cook until thick enough to stand when cut. Pour into the baked pie shell. In a small mixing bowl beat the egg whites until stiff but not dry. Gradually beat in 3 tablespoons of sugar. Spoon the meringue over the pie, pushing to the edges of the crust to seal. Bake at 325° for 10 minutes, or until brown.
Yield: 8 servings.

Amber Pie

3 egg yolks
1 cup sugar
1 tablespoon butter
2 tablespoons all-purpose flour
½ teaspoon cinnamon
¼ teaspoon cloves
¼ teaspoon allspice
¼ teaspoon nutmeg
1 cup buttermilk
½ cup raisins
½ cup pecan pieces
1 unbaked 9-inch pie shell

In a medium bowl cream the egg yolks, sugar, and butter until light and fluffy. Add the remaining ingredients except the pie shell and blend until smooth. Pour into the pie shell. Bake at 325° for 35 to 40 minutes, or until firm in the center. May be served warm or cold.
Yield: 6 to 8 servings.

James Beard House, New York City

In 1990, Lynne and I took Mary Ruth Hall with us to the James Beard House in New York City to host a Miss Mary Bobo's Boarding House mid-day dinner for the James Beard Foundation. James Beard profoundly influenced American cooking, so it was fitting to present a typical American meal such as Miss Mary would have prepared. The major-domo at the house had purchased green beans for dinner as we had requested, but when we arrived the day before with our cook, we found that the beans were an oriental variety. We had just enough time to exchange them for country-style green beans before we went out for a big evening of dining and theater. We returned from our festivities only to string beans at midnight so they would be ready to cook the next morning. This event was quite a success, and later we returned to the Beard House for two other southern events, a Tennessee barbecue and a Jack Daniel's birthday celebration dinner.

Fresh Strawberry Pie

Tennessee produces beautiful strawberries, so it stands to reason that this luscious fruit is showcased in this wonderful pie.

2 cups fresh, ripe strawberries, divided
1 baked 9-inch pie shell
1 cup sugar
2 tablespoons cornstarch
Pinch salt
1 8-ounce carton whipping cream
¼ cup sugar

Slice 1 cup of strawberries in half and place them in the baked pie crust. In a medium saucepan crush the remaining strawberries with a fork or potato masher and place over medium heat. Bring to boiling, add 1 cup of sugar, the cornstarch, and salt. Cook until thick, about 5 minutes. Cool and then spoon over the berries in the pie crust. Chill in the refrigerator.

To serve, whip the cream with the remaining ¼ cup of sugar, top the pie, slice, and serve.
Yield: 6 to 8 servings.

Syrup Pie

½ cup sugar
1 cup dark cane syrup
¼ teaspoon baking soda
Pinch of salt
½ cup butter
3 eggs, beaten
1 tablespoon flour
Fresh orange peel, grated
¼ cup Jack Daniel's Whiskey
1 9-inch unbaked pie crust

In a saucepan mix sugar, syrup, soda, and salt. Bring to a boil, then remove from heat and cool. Stir in butter, beaten eggs, flour, orange peel, and Jack Daniel's Whiskey. Pour into unbaked pie crust. Bake at 325° for 50 minutes or until firm in center.
Yield: 6 to 8 servings.

Desserts

Topsy-Turvy Tennessee Peach Pudding

½ cup sugar
1 cup all-purpose flour
2 teaspoons baking powder
½ teaspoon salt
½ cup milk
2 cups fresh Tennessee peaches, diced
½ cup sugar
½ cup brown sugar
2 cups water
1 tablespoon butter
¼ teaspoon nutmeg

In a large bowl stir together ½ cup of sugar, the flour, baking powder, and salt. Add milk and then peaches. Stir gently to mix, and spread in a well-buttered 8-inch square pan.

In a saucepan combine the remaining sugars, water, butter, and nutmeg. Heat the mixture to boiling, stirring to dissolve the sugars. Carefully pour the mixture over the batter in the baking dish. Bake at 400° for 40 to 50 minutes.

This may be served hot or cold. Spoon into dessert dishes and pass a pitcher of light cream to pour over the top.
Yield: 6 servings.

Tennessee Peach Cobbler

Pastry

1 cup self-rising flour
½ teaspoon salt
⅓ cup lard or shortening
4 tablespoons milk

Filling

8 large peaches, peeled and sliced
1¾ cups sugar
½ teaspoon cinnamon
½ cup butter, cut into pats

In a mixing bowl place flour and salt, cut in lard to resemble coarse corn meal. Add milk and stir to make dough. Place on floured board and roll out to ¼-inch thickness. Cut into long strips. Butter sides and bottom of 9 x 13-inch baking dish. Place some strips of pastry lengthwise of the baking dish. Add the peach slices, and sprinkle 1½ cups sugar over. Lattice the remaining pastry strips across the top of peaches. Sprinkle the top with the remaining ¼ cup sugar and cinnamon and dot top with butter patties. Bake at 350° for 35 to 40 minutes. Top will be golden and crusty. Delicious as is, or top with cream!
Yield: 6 to 8 servings.

Eady's Woodforth Pudding

This is commonly known as Woodford Pudding, but Eady always referred to it as "Woodforth," so we do too.

3 eggs, beaten
1 cup sugar
½ cup butter, softened
1 cup all-purpose flour
1 cup blackberry jam
1 teaspoon cinnamon
1 teaspoon vanilla extract
1 teaspoon baking soda
3 tablespoons buttermilk

In a large mixing bowl combine the ingredients, adding one at a time in the order listed. Pour into a buttered 13 x 9-inch baking dish. Bake at 350° for 30 minutes. The center will spring back when touched. Should be served while warm with sauce spooned over the top.

Lynchburg Lemon Sauce

½ cup sugar
2 tablespoons cornstarch
¼ teaspoon salt
2 cups water
½ cup butter
1 tablespoon grated lemon rind
3 tablespoons lemon juice
Jack Daniel's Whiskey

In a saucepan combine the sugar, cornstarch, and salt. Add the water gradually. Cook over medium heat until the mixture boils, stirring constantly. Continue to stir and boil for 1 minute longer, then remove the pan from the heat. Stir in the butter, lemon rind, and lemon juice. Before serving, stir in Jack Daniel's Whiskey to taste.
Yield: 8 servings.

Old-Time Steamed Pudding

¾ cup boiling water
1 cup raisins, chopped
3 tablespoons shortening
¼ cup Jack Daniel's Whiskey
½ cup sugar
½ cup molasses
1 egg, beaten
1½ cups all-purpose flour, sifted
1 teaspoon baking soda
1 teaspoon salt

In a small bowl pour the boiling water over the raisins and shortening. In a large bowl combine the Jack Daniel's Whiskey, sugar, and molasses. Add the beaten egg. In a separate bowl combine the dry ingredients and add them to the batter. Stir in the raisins. Carefully grease a 1-quart mold and fill it with the batter. Place lid on steamer; place in a pan of hot water and steam at 325° for 2 hours. Serve hot with The Gentleman's Sauce (see page 142) spooned over the top.
Yield: 6 to 8 servings.

Toffee-Topped Chocolate Pudding

½ cup butter, melted
2 cups sugar
1 teaspoon vanilla extract
6 tablespoons cocoa
4 eggs, slightly beaten
1 cup all-purpose flour
Pinch of salt
½ cup pecan pieces

In a bowl cream the butter and sugar until light and fluffy. Add the vanilla and cocoa, then the eggs. Stir in the flour, salt, and pecans. Pour the pudding into an ungreased 8-inch square pan. Place the pan into a larger pan of hot water. Bake at 325° for 40 minutes. While the pudding bakes prepare the topping.

Toffee Topping

1 cup light brown sugar
6 tablespoons cream
½ cup butter
¼ cup Jack Daniel's Whiskey
Whipped cream or ice cream (optional)

In a saucepan combine all of the ingredients and bring the mixture to a boil. Lower the heat and simmer for 3 minutes. Remove the pan from the heat. After the pudding is done, pour the topping over it. Return the pudding to the oven for 5 minutes, until the topping bubbles and browns.

Cool and serve topped with whipped cream or ice cream, if desired.
Yield: 6 to 8 servings.

Sweet Potato Pudding with Tennessee Whiskey Sauce

¼ cup butter
½ cup sugar
¼ cup firmly packed brown sugar
2 eggs, beaten
1 teaspoon cinnamon
¼ teaspoon nutmeg
¼ teaspoon cloves
Dash of salt
2½ cups uncooked sweet potatoes, shredded
1½ cups milk
Whipped cream

In a large mixing bowl cream butter and sugars; beat eggs into sugar mixture. Add spices and salt. Stir potatoes into sugar mixture; add milk and mix thoroughly. Pour into a greased 2-quart baking dish. Bake at 400° for 50 to 60 minutes. To serve, spoon Tennessee Whiskey Sauce over and top with whipped cream.
Yield: 6 to 8 servings.

Tennessee Whiskey Sauce

1¼ cups water
½ cup firmly packed light brown sugar
¼ teaspoon nutmeg
¼ cup Jack Daniel's Whiskey
1½ tablespoons cornstarch
2 tablespoons butter

In a small saucepan combine water, sugar, and nutmeg. Bring to a boil. Combine Jack Daniel's Whiskey and cornstarch; stir into sugar mixture. Cook until thickened. Blend in butter until melted.
Yield: 1¼ cups.

Mary Ruth Hall, Lynchburg Hostess

Mary Ruth Hall, the hostess at the table, lived at the boarding house when she worked as Lynchburg's county extension agent. She paid $12.50 a week for room and board. Now she gets *paid to eat good food and host a dinner table full of interesting guests. Times have changed!*

Photo by Hope Powell

Country Bread Pudding with Tennessee Blackberry Topping

Butter
8 stale biscuits
1 cup sugar
3 eggs, slightly beaten
1½ cups milk
2 tablespoons lemon extract
Dash salt

Butter generously the bottom and sides of a 17 x 11-inch baking dish. Crumble the stale biscuits into the dish. In a medium mixing bowl combine the sugar, eggs, milk, lemon extract, and salt. Stir to blend well. Pour the mixture over the crumbled biscuits. This should be soupy. Add ¼ cup more of milk if needed (country biscuits tend to be larger than the small ones that people make today). Bake at 350° for 30 minutes. The custard will be set and lightly brown. Serve hot or cold with Tennessee Blackberry Topping and pass a pitcher of cream, if desired.

Tennessee Blackberry Topping

2 cups fresh or thawed frozen blackberries
2 teaspoons cornstarch
2 tablespoons lemon juice
½ cup white grape juice
⅓ cup Jack Daniel's Whiskey, divided

In a medium saucepan mash 1 cup of the berries. Dissolve the cornstarch in the lemon juice; add to the berries along with the grape juice and half of the Jack Daniel's Whiskey. Heat until thickened and clear. Add the remaining whole berries and warm through. In a separate saucepan heat the remaining Jack Daniel's Whiskey; pour over warm blackberries and carefully ignite. Spoon over Country Bread Pudding.
Yield: 10 servings.

Country Blackberry Roll

¾ cup sugar
2 cups blackberries
2 cups flour
1 teaspoon salt
2 teaspoons sugar
½ cup butter, softened
1 egg, beaten
⅓ cup milk

In a medium mixing bowl sprinkle sugar over the blackberries and gently stir to cover. In another bowl sift dry ingredients and add ⅓ cup butter (room temperature); cut into the dry ingredients with a knife. Add the egg and milk to make a soft dough. Turn dough onto a floured bread board and knead lightly to hold dough together. Roll out to ¼-inch thickness and spread remaining butter over top. Spoon sweetened blackberries over dough and then roll up, jelly-roll fashion. Place on baking sheet and bake at 400° for 25 minutes. Serve warm or cold; slice and serve with ice cream.
Yield: 6 servings.

Official invitation to the American Festival Cafe's gala party to kick off the six-week tribute to Miss Mary Bobo's Boarding House.

Coconut Custard with Caramel Topping

Butter (or margarine)
½ cup sugar
½ cup boiling water
6 eggs
¾ cups sugar
½ teaspoon salt
4 cups milk, scalded
½ teaspoon vanilla extract
½ cup coconut

Brush a heavy skillet lightly with butter. Add the sugar and cook over medium high heat, stirring constantly, until the sugar melts and becomes golden brown in color. Slowly add the boiling water, stirring until the sugar is dissolved. Remove the pan from the heat and cool.

In a large mixing bowl beat the eggs with a rotary beater. Add the sugar, salt, milk, and vanilla, stirring to blend completely. Stir in the coconut. Butter 8 custard cups and place 2 tablespoons of the caramelized syrup in each cup. Carefully spoon the coconut custard over the syrup. Place in a baking dish large enough to hold all 8 cups. Add water to the baking dish to come halfway up the sides of the cups. Bake at 325° for 30 to 40 minutes, until a cake tester or knife inserted in center comes out only slightly coated. The custards will continue to cook after they are removed from the oven.

Serve hot or cold in cups or removed to dessert dishes.
Yield: 8 servings.

American Festival Cafe Gala

The American Festival Cafe at Rockefeller Center in New York City had a six-week tribute to Miss Mary Bobo's Boarding House by offering a boarding house meal to its guests, using recipes from our cookbooks. The event was to run for six weeks, but it was so successful that it was extended to eight weeks. A big press party was the kick-off and Lynne, Mary Ruth (one of the Lynchburg hostesses), and I went to New York for the gala. It was a wonderful party, and Miss Mary was there in spirit, not only because her picture was placed prominently at the entrance, but also because of the foods that were served. Many items from the boarding house were put on display in cases throughout the restaurant. The cases here highlight photos, a soup tureen, vanity items, a butter churn, a Tennessee sunbonnet, and an oil lamp. Many guests acknowledged that this was their first experience with country-fried steak. Imagine that!

Apricot Prune Tart

1 cup dried prunes
1 cup dried apricots
½ cup sugar
1 tablespoon lemon juice
1 cup plus 1 tablespoon buttermilk
1 teaspoon baking soda
2⅓ cups all-purpose flour
1¾ cups sugar
1 teaspoon salt
1 teaspoon nutmeg
1 teaspoon cinnamon
3 eggs
1 cup plus 1 tablespoon melted butter
1 teaspoon vanilla extract
1 cup pecans, chopped

In a large saucepan combine the dried prunes and apricots and cook with water to cover. Add ½ cup of sugar and the lemon juice and cook to the mushy pulp stage. Stir often and be careful not to burn. Lower the heat if necessary. Set aside to cool.

In a small bowl combine the buttermilk with the soda. In a large bowl combine the flour, sugar, salt, and spices. In a medium bowl beat the eggs, melted butter, and vanilla and add the egg mixture to the dry ingredients. Stir in the buttermilk and blend until smooth. Stir in the fruit mixture and nuts. Pour into 2 buttered 9-inch cake pans. Bake at 350° for 40 minutes.

While the tarts bake, prepare the topping.

Topping

½ cup butter, melted
½ teaspoon baking soda
⅔ cup buttermilk
1 cup sugar

In a saucepan combine all of the ingredients and bring to a rolling boil. Pour the hot mixture over the tarts when removed from the oven. Cut each tart into 8 slices. Cool and then chill in the refrigerator with foil covering.

This is an excellent dessert to prepare the day before an event.
Yield: 16 servings.

Real Banana Pudding

This is a forever favorite with everyone.

½ cup sugar
⅓ cup all-purpose flour
¼ teaspoon salt
2 cups milk
4 eggs, separated
1 teaspoon vanilla extract
1 12 ounce box vanilla wafers
6 bananas
6 tablespoons sugar

In the top of a double boiler combine the sugar, flour, and salt. Add the milk. Separate the egg yolks and slightly beat with a fork; stir into mixture. Place the pan over boiling water and cook until the consistency of thick custard. Stir in the vanilla.

Line a glass baking dish with vanilla wafers. Slice bananas over wafers. Pour half of the custard over the bananas. Repeat.

In a small bowl, beat the egg whites with an electric mixer on high. Add the sugar and beat until stiff peaks form. Spoon over the top of the pudding. Bake at 425° until the top is golden brown.
Yield: 8 servings

Old South Butter Cups

These are delicious lemon puddings from the historic moments of Miss Mary's table fare.

1 cup sugar
¼ cup all-purpose flour
½ teaspoon salt
¾ cup butter, melted
5 tablespoons lemon juice
Grated rind of one lemon
3 eggs, separated
1½ cups milk

In a medium bowl blend the sugar, flour, and salt. Add the butter, lemon juice, and rind, stirring to blend well. Add the beaten egg yolks and milk and mix well. In a separate bowl beat the egg whites until stiff and glossy but not dry. Fold the egg whites into the pudding mixture. Pour into 8 buttered custard cups. Place the cups in a pan with hot water about 1 inch deep. Bake at 325° for 40 to 45 minutes. Remove and cool to serve. *Yield: 8 servings.*

Old-Fashioned Shortcakes

2 cups all-purpose flour
1 tablespoon sugar
2 teaspoons baking powder
¼ teaspoon salt
¼ cup butter
¾ cup milk

In a large bowl combine the dry ingredients. Add the butter and cut into dry ingredients with a knife or pastry cutter. The mixture will resemble coarsely ground meal. Stir in the milk. Turn the dough onto a lightly floured board. Knead the dough slightly and roll it to ½-inch thickness. With a biscuit cutter or 2-inch glass, cut out 6 rounds of shortcake and place them on a lightly greased cookie sheet. Bake at 450° for 20 minutes or until a light golden brown. Remove from the oven and place on racks to cool.

Fresh Strawberries and Cream Topping

1 quart fresh, ripe strawberries
⅓ cup sugar
½ pint cold whipping cream
2 tablespoons sugar
1 teaspoon vanilla extract

Wash and hull the strawberries, then slice. Sprinkle ⅓ cup of sugar over the strawberries, cover with plastic wrap, and refrigerate until serving time. Stir before serving.

At serving time, whip the whipping cream, gradually adding 2 tablespoons of sugar and the vanilla.

Split each shortcake, placing the bottom half on serving plates. Spoon the strawberries over each shortcake. Top with other half of the shortcake and repeat with the strawberries. Add a generous dollop of the whipped cream, serve, and enjoy! *Yield: 6 servings.*

Clarence Rolman's 90th Birthday Celebration

(L-R) Pat, Clarence, Mary Eady, his daughter, and Lynne

You Are Invited To Attend
A Party When

Jack Daniel Distillery

Recognizes

Tennessee Squire and Goodwill Ambassador

Clarence Rolman

on his 90th Birthday

February 10, 1992
Miss Mary Bobo's Boarding House
Lynchburg, Tennessee
2:00 p.m. — 5:00 p.m.

Clarence Rolman began working for the Jack Daniel Distillery after prohibition in 1938. After he retired, he worked as a tour guide at the distillery's visitor center. Clarence then became the distillery's first Goodwill Ambassador. He and his late wife, Elvie, traveled all over the United States, Canada, Australia, New Zealand, and the United Kingdom spreading goodwill and making friends for Lynchburg and Jack Daniel's. Miss Mary's Boarding House has always been the hub of hospitality in Lynchburg, and so on Clarence's 90th birthday, more than one hundred well-wishers came by for the special celebration held in his honor.

Photo by Hope Powell

Tipsy Pudding

3 eggs
6 tablespoons sugar
¾ cup all-purpose flour
Butter
Sugar
¾ cup Jack Daniel's Whiskey
Shredded coconut
Whipped cream (optional)

In a medium bowl beat the eggs and sugar until thick and lemon colored. Stir in the flour lightly. Butter 6 ovenproof custard cups and coat with sugar. Fill each cup ¾ full with pudding. Bake at 350° for 20 minutes, or until set. Remove the pudding from the oven and pour 2 tablespoons of Jack Daniel's Whiskey over each. Sprinkle lightly with shredded coconut. Cool and then refrigerate. Serve cold with whipped cream, if desired.
Yield: 6 servings.

Blueberry Buckle

½ cup shortening
1 cup sugar, divided
1 egg, beaten
2½ cups flour, divided
2½ teaspoons soda
¼ teaspoon salt
½ cup milk
2 cups fresh blueberries
¼ cup butter

In a mixing bowl cream shortening and ½ cup of sugar. Add beaten egg and stir to mix. Add 2 cups flour, soda, and salt alternately with the milk, stirring to blend. Butter an 8-inch square baking dish (can add wax paper to bottom to assist removal and to serve). Spoon the batter into the prepared dish. Sprinkle blueberries over the top of batter. In a small bowl combine the remaining sugar, flour, and butter until crumbly and sprinkle over the blueberries. Bake at 375° for one hour and 15 minutes. Can be served plain or with cream.
Yield: 8 servings.

Tennessee Fresh Apple Betty

6 to 8 fresh apples, peeled, cored, and sliced
¼ cup sugar
¼ cup water
2 tablespoons flour
½ teaspoon cinnamon
1 cup oatmeal
¼ cup brown sugar, firmly packed
¼ cup butter
¼ teaspoon cinnamon

In a large bowl combine the apples, sugar, water, flour, and ½ teaspoon of cinnamon. Spoon into a 9-inch square baking dish.

In a small bowl combine the oatmeal, brown sugar, butter, and remaining cinnamon and spoon over apples. Bake at 350° for 45 minutes, or until fruit is tender and topping is crusty.

Delicious topped with ice cream or with whipped cream.
Yield: 8 servings.

Rhubarb Crisp

1 cup oatmeal
1¾ cups all-purpose flour, divided
1 cup shortening
1 cup brown sugar
4½ cups raw rhubarb, finely cut
½ teaspoon red food coloring
1½ cups sugar
Pinch salt

Combine the oatmeal, 1½ cups of flour, the shortening, and brown sugar and blend as for a pie crust (this will be coarse in texture). Spread ¾ of the mixture over the bottom of a buttered 13 x 9-inch baking dish. Combine the remaining flour, rhubarb, food coloring, sugar, and salt. Spoon the mixture over the crust mixture. Top with the remaining crust mixture. Bake at 350° for 40 minutes. Increase the oven temperature to 400° and continue to bake for 15 minutes. Remove the crisp from the oven. Serve hot or cold with a pitcher of cream to pour over, if desired.
Yield: 15 servings.

Royal Bananas

These are so called because they are really fit for a king!

3 firm bananas
3 tablespoons butter
⅓ cup light brown sugar, firmly packed
Dash nutmeg
Dash cinnamon
¼ cup Jack Daniel's Whiskey
Vanilla ice cream

Peel the bananas and cut into 2-inch slices. In a large skillet over medium heat melt the butter. Add the sugar and spices and stir until melted. Place the banana slices in the skillet and cook until tender. Remove the skillet from the heat. Add the Jack Daniel's Whiskey and carefully ignite. Serve hot over ice cream.
Yield: 6 servings.

Poached Peaches in Jack

½ cup sugar
½ cup Jack Daniel's Whiskey
1 cup water
4 large peaches, peeled
⅓ cup heavy cream
¼ teaspoon vanilla extract

In a saucepan combine the sugar, Jack Daniel's Whiskey, and water and bring the mixture to a boil over high heat. Add the peaches. Reduce the heat to medium high and poach the peaches, turning frequently until tender, about 10 to 12 minutes. Remove the pan from the heat; lift the peaches out of the liquid and place them in a bowl. Return the saucepan to the heat and boil until reduced by half. Pour the liquid over the peaches and cool to room temperature. Refrigerate covered.

In a medium bowl whip the cream with the vanilla until stiff. To serve, slice the peaches in half and remove the pits. Place 2 peach halves in each dessert dish and top with a large dollop of whipped cream.
Yield: 4 servings.

Table Hostesses

(L-R) Mary Katherine Holt, Mary Ruth Hall, Mary Holt, and Margaret Tolley

These table hostesses pose for a picture in front of the house after dinner. Each table is hosted by a lovely lady from Lynchburg. The ladies say they have the best job in town. Consider the perks: they eat a dinner that has been prepared by the best of cooks, laugh a lot, enjoy the meal with twelve to fifteen guests, and leave without having to clean up. And if that's not enough, they get paid for their trouble!

Photo by Hope Powell

Tennessee Peaches and Cream

2 large ripe Tennessee peaches
¼ cup Jack Daniel's Whiskey
¼ cup brown sugar, firmly packed
4 pats butter
Vanilla ice cream

In a greased pan place the peach halves with cut side up. In each cavity place 1 tablespoon of Jack Daniel's Whiskey, 1 tablespoon of sugar, and one pat of butter. Bake at 325° for 20 to 25 minutes or until the peaches are tender. Serve warm with a scoop of vanilla ice cream.
Yield: 4 servings.

Southern Rice Pudding

3 eggs
1 cup sugar
2 cups milk
1½ teaspoons cornstarch
½ teaspoon vanilla extract
⅓ cup rice, cooked and cooled
Raisins (optional)
Nutmeg

In a medium bowl beat the eggs until light and lemon-colored. Add the sugar and mix well. Add the milk, cornstarch, and vanilla and mix well. Add the cooked rice and raisins. Pour into a buttered 1½-quart baking dish and sprinkle the top with nutmeg. Place the baking dish in a pan of hot water about 1-inch deep. Bake at 325° for 60 minutes, or until the custard is set.
Yield: 8 servings.

Tennessee Raisin Roll

1 cup raisins
⅓ cup butter, melted
1 cup sugar
1 teaspoon cinnamon
½ cup pecans, chopped
Pastry for a 9-inch pie (use your favorite recipe)
1 cup sugar
½ teaspoon baking soda
½ cup buttermilk
1 tablespoon light corn syrup
½ cup butter
¼ cup Jack Daniel's Whiskey

Plump raisins in enough boiling water to cover. Drain. In a small bowl combine the raisins, butter, sugar, cinnamon, and pecans. Set aside.

Roll the pastry into a rectangular shape. Spread the raisin filling evenly over the entire surface. Roll the pastry in a jelly-roll fashion, starting with the narrow side. Gently place on a greased cookie sheet. Bake at 375° for 30 minutes or until golden brown. While the roll bakes, prepared the sauce.

In a saucepan combine the remaining ingredients except the Jack Daniel's Whiskey. Bring to a boil over medium heat and cook until the soft ball (235°) stage. Remove the pan from the heat. Cool. Stir Jack Daniel's Whiskey into the sauce and blend. To serve, slice the raisin roll and place slices on serving plates. Pour sauce over the slices and serve. This may be topped with whipped cream, if desired.
Yield: 8 to 10 servings.

Two Friendly Faces

Velma (left) was known as the singing cook. Her fried chicken was melt-in-your-mouth wonderful. It was the kind of chicken that made southern fried chicken truly famous. Just before this book went to press, Velma passed away. Her cooking, her singing, and her sweet disposition are sorely missed. Barbara (right), here helping serve at a table, is a queen of all trades helping in whatever capacity is needed. Her outstanding work and her congenial attitude are just two of her noteworthy attributes.

Tennessee Sundae

1 cup candied cherries
1 cup pecans, chopped
½ cup Jack Daniel's Whiskey
½ gallon vanilla ice cream
1 cup coconut macaroons, crumbled
Maraschino cherries (optional)
Coconut macaroons for garnish

Soak the cherries and pecans in Jack Daniel's Whiskey overnight or for several hours. Remove the ice cream from the carton and let it soften just enough to fold in the cherry mixture along with the crumbled macaroons. Return the ice cream to a large container and refreeze. At serving time, spoon into dessert dishes. Top with a maraschino cherry and a whole macaroon, if desired.
Yield: 12 to 14 servings.

Lemon Cream on a Cloud

4 egg whites
1 cup sugar
¼ teaspoon cream of tartar
4 egg yolks, beaten
½ cup sugar
3 tablespoons lemon juice
1 tablespoon lemon rind, finely grated
1 pint cold whipping cream

In a medium bowl beat the egg whites until stiff but not dry. Gradually add the sugar and cream of tartar, beating until smooth and glossy. Spread the meringue on the bottom and sides of a well-greased 10-inch pan, indenting the center of the meringue slightly and raising up on the sides, being careful not to push to the edge of the rim. Bake at 275° for 1 hour. Cool completely.

In the top of a double boiler, stir together the egg yolks, sugar, lemon juice, and rind. Cook over hot water, stirring until very thick, about 10 minutes. Remove from heat and cool.

Whip the whipping cream until stiff and peaks form. Fold it into the cooled lemon cream. Spoon the filling into the meringue cloud and serve.

This may be made one day ahead and covered to refrigerate until serving time.
Yield: 8 servings.

Jam Strudel

1 cup butter
2 cups all-purpose flour
½ tablespoon salt
½ cup sour cream
1 10-ounce jar apricot, peach, or strawberry jam
1 cup coconut, shredded
⅔ cup walnuts, chopped
Confectioners' sugar

In a bowl blend the butter, flour, and salt with a pastry cutter, as for pie crust. Mix in the sour cream and place in the refrigerator overnight.

Remove the dough from the refrigerator and allow it to come to room temperature. Divide the dough into 2 balls. Roll the first ball into a rectangle 10 x 15 inches. Spread with half the jam; top with half the coconut and half the walnuts. Roll up jelly-roll fashion. Repeat with the second ball of dough.

Place the rolls on a greased 10 x 15-inch baking sheet. Bake at 350° for 1 hour, or until golden brown. Remove from the oven and let cool for 10 minutes. Cut into pieces and sprinkle with confectioners' sugar to serve.
Yield: 18 servings.

Southern Bar Cookies

1 cup butter
1½ cups sugar
3 eggs, slightly beaten
¼ cup Jack Daniel's Whiskey
2 cups all-purpose flour
½ teaspoon baking soda
1 teaspoon nutmeg
1 teaspoon cinnamon
1½ cups raisins
½ cup pecans, chopped
½ cup confectioners' sugar
2 tablespoons Jack Daniel's Whiskey

In a large bowl cream the butter and 1½ cups of sugar. Add the eggs and ¼ cup of Jack Daniel's Whiskey. In a separate bowl combine 1½ cups of flour, the baking soda, and spices. Sprinkle ½ cup of flour mixture over the raisins and pecans. When the dough is well blended, add the raisin mixture and mix well. Grease a 9-inch square pan and spread the dough to cover the pan bottom. Bake at 375° for 10 to 12 minutes. Remove and cut into diamond-shaped bars. In a small shallow bowl combine the confectioners' sugar and remaining Jack Daniel's Whiskey. Gently roll the hot cookies in the sugar mixture to coat. Remove to a rack to cool.
Yield: 2 dozen cookies.

Belle of Lincoln Spice Cookies

¾ cup sugar
4 tablespoons Jack Daniel's Whiskey
¾ cup butter, softened
1 cup brown sugar
1 egg
¼ cup molasses
2½ cups all-purpose flour
½ teaspoon salt
¾ teaspoon ginger
1½ teaspoons cinnamon
¼ teaspoon cloves
¼ teaspoon baking soda
1½ teaspoons baking powder

In a small bowl mix ¾ cup of sugar and the Jack Daniel's Whiskey. Set the bowl aside.

In a large bowl cream the butter and brown sugar with an electric mixer on medium high. Add the egg and molasses and blend well. In a separate bowl combine all of the dry ingredients. With the mixer on low, gradually add the dry ingredients to the batter. When just mixed, cover the dough and chill in the refrigerator.

Stir the sugar and Jack Daniel's Whiskey mixture to keep blended.

After the dough has chilled (about 1 hour), remove and pinch off pieces slightly smaller than a Ping-Pong ball. Roll the balls in the flavored sugar and place on a lightly greased cookie sheet. With the back of a spoon flatten the top of each cookie and place one drop of Jack Daniel's Whiskey on top. Bake at 375° for 10 to 12 minutes. Remove from oven and cool on racks.
Yield: 5 dozen.

Dinner Guests at Table

After dinner, guests linger to chat with the new friends they have made. The hostess here is Mrs. Coble, who for many years taught school in Lynchburg. She was loved by every student who sat in her classes. For the past few years she has been unable to continue hostessing a table, but her conversation was always fun and stimulating for the diners. A meal such as this invites all to relax and enjoy the table and conversation instead of rushing headlong into the remainder of the day.

Tipsy Spice Cookies

1/4 cup Jack Daniel's Whiskey
1 cup raisins
1 8-ounce package chopped dates
1 cup butter, softened
1 1/2 cups sugar
3 eggs
3 cups all-purpose flour
1 teaspoon baking soda
1 1/2 teaspoons cinnamon
1/4 teaspoon salt
1/2 teaspoon nutmeg
1/2 teaspoon cloves

In a small bowl pour the Jack Daniel's Whiskey over the raisins and dates. Set the bowl aside to soak for 1 hour.

In a separate bowl cream the butter and sugar until light and fluffy. Add the eggs one at a time, beating well after each addition. In a separate bowl combine the dry ingredients, then stir the mixture into the batter. Stir in the fruit mixture and nuts. Blend well. Drop the dough by teaspoons onto a greased cookie sheet. Bake at 350° for 12 to 15 minutes, until lightly browned.
Yield: 6 dozen.

Tennessee Toffee Cookies

1 cup butter, softened
1 cup sugar
1 egg, separated
1 teaspoon vanilla extract
3 teaspoons Jack Daniel's Whiskey
1 3/4 cups all-purpose flour, sifted
1/2 cup pecans, broken

In a bowl cream the butter and sugar until light and fluffy. Stir in the egg yolk, vanilla, and Jack Daniel's Whiskey. Add the flour a little at a time until well blended. Spread the dough very thinly on a greased cookie sheet. Place a sheet of waxed paper over it and roll the dough with a rolling pin to spread evenly on the cookie sheet. Beat the egg white with a mixer until foamy. Spread the egg white over the top of the cookie dough and sprinkle with pecan pieces. Bake at 250° for 55 minutes. Remove from the oven and cut into diagonal cookies immediately before they cool. To remove after they cool, cut again.

A delightful holiday treat!
Yield: 2 dozen.

Potato Chip Shortbread Cookies

2 cups butter, softened
1 cup sugar
2 teaspoons vanilla extract
3 cups all-purpose flour
1 cup pecans, chopped
2 cups potato chips (unflavored), crushed
2 cups confectioners' sugar, sifted

In a large bowl cream the butter, sugar, and vanilla with an electric mixer until light and fluffy. Add the flour and mix well. Stir in the nuts and crushed potato chips. Drop by the teaspoon onto a greased cookie sheet. Bake at 350° for 10 to 15 minutes or until golden brown. Remove from the pan and roll in confectioners' sugar. Cool on racks.
Yield: 4 dozen.

Moore County Hermits

¼ cup shortening
1 cup sugar
1 egg
¼ cup molasses
1 cup raisins
2¾ cups all-purpose flour
2 teaspoons salt
½ teaspoon cinnamon
½ teaspoon nutmeg
¼ cup Jack Daniel's Whiskey

In a large bowl cream the shortening and sugar until light and fluffy. Beat in the egg and molasses. In a separate bowl combine the raisins with the dry ingredients, coating them with the flour. Stir the dry ingredients into the egg mixture alternately with the Jack Daniel's Whiskey. Cover the dough and chill it in the refrigerator. (The dough may be made ahead and stored for 3 or 4 days to bake later.)

Divide the dough into 3 portions. Roll the first ball on a lightly floured bread board to a 13 x 9-inch rectangle. Beginning at the narrow side, roll up jelly-roll fashion. The log will be about 1 inch in diameter. Repeat with the other 2 balls of dough. Place each log on a greased cookie sheet, being careful that the logs do not touch. Sprinkle the tops of the logs with sugar.

Bake at 350° for 15 to 18 minutes. Do not overbake. The logs are done when no imprint lingers when pressed with a finger. Remove from the oven and cut into 1-inch bars. Roll in extra sugar (or confectioners' sugar) while hot, if desired. Cool on a wire rack.
Yield: 3 dozen.

Lemon Meringue Squares

½ cup butter, softened
½ cup confectioners' sugar
2 egg yolks
1 cup all-purpose flour
2 teaspoons lemon rind, finely grated
½ teaspoon salt

In a medium bowl cream together the butter and sugar. Add the egg yolks and blend. Stir in the flour, lemon rind, and salt. Spread the batter in an ungreased 13 x 9-inch baking dish. Bake at 350° for 10 minutes. While the cake bakes prepare the topping.

Topping

2 egg whites
½ cup sugar
1 tablespoon lemon juice
½ cup pecans, chopped

In a small bowl beat the egg whites until stiff. Gradually add the sugar and lemon juice and fold in the pecans.

When the cake has baked for 10 minutes, remove it from the oven and spread the topping over the hot, partially baked batter. Return the pan to the oven and continue to bake for 25 minutes. Cool completely and cut into squares. Serve with a generous scoop of vanilla ice cream.
Yield: 8 servings.

Tennessee Cranberry Cookies

1 cup unsalted butter, softened
1 cup sugar
1 large egg
3 cups all-purpose flour
⅓ cup Jack Daniel's Whiskey
½ cup dried cranberries (see note below)
1 egg, lightly beaten
4 tablespoons cream

In a large bowl cream together the butter and sugar. Add the egg, flour, Jack Daniel's Whiskey, and cranberries, mixing well. On a lightly floured board roll the dough ¼-inch thick and cut with a biscuit cutter or small glass. Place on a greased cookie sheet. In a small bowl mix together quickly with a fork the beaten egg and cream and brush the tops of the cookies. Bake at 350° for 10 to 15 minutes. Remove and cool on racks.

Note: Dried cranberries may be purchased in specialty food markets.
Yield: 6 dozen.

Miss Mary's Ginger Snaps

½ cup butter, softened
1 cup sugar
2 eggs, slightly beaten
½ cup molasses
4½ cups all-purpose flour
3 teaspoons ginger
1 teaspoon salt
1 teaspoon baking soda
Confectioners' sugar

In a large bowl cream the butter and sugar together until light and fluffy. Add the eggs and molasses. Combine the dry ingredients (except confectioners' sugar) and add to the butter mixture. Cover the bowl and place in the refrigerator to chill.

On a bread board sift confectioners' sugar to cover. Place the chilled cookie dough on the board and roll out until thin. Cut the cookies with a cookie or biscuit cutter. Place on lightly greased cookie sheets. Bake at 400° for 15 minutes. Remove from the pans and cool on racks.
Yield: 3 dozen.

Pecan Icebox Cookies

1 cup butter (do not use margarine)
2¼ cups light brown sugar
⅓ cup sugar
2 eggs
1 teaspoon vanilla extract
3 cups all-purpose flour
½ teaspoon baking soda
2 cups pecans, finely ground (use food processor)

In a large bowl cream the butter and sugars with an electric mixer until fluffy. Add the eggs and vanilla and mix well. In a separate bowl stir the flour and baking soda together and add the mixture to the batter. Stir in the ground pecans. Form the dough into rolls on wax paper and refrigerate for at least 12 hours. Slice thin and place on ungreased cookie sheets. Bake at 350° for 8 to 10 minutes.
Yield: 6 dozen.

Jack Daniel's Caramel Sauce

1 cup sugar
½ cup buttermilk
½ cup butter
½ teaspoon baking soda
1 tablespoon light corn syrup
¼ cup Jack Daniel's Whiskey

In a saucepan combine the sugar, buttermilk, and butter. Bring the mixture to a boil, stirring constantly. Boil for several minutes, until the sugar is melted and the mixture has thickened. Remove the pan from the heat and cool slightly. Add the baking soda and corn syrup. Set aside to cool until serving time. At serving time, stir in the Jack Daniel's Whiskey and spoon over the chess squares.
Yield: 15 servings.

Delicious Chess Squares

1 cup butter
1 box light brown sugar
½ cup sugar
4 eggs
2 cups all-purpose flour
1 teaspoon baking powder
1 teaspoon vanilla extract
 Pinch salt
1 cup pecans, chopped

In a saucepan heat the butter and brown sugar over low heat. Remove the pan from the heat and add the remaining ingredients. Mix well and pour into a 13 x 9-inch greased and floured cake pan. Bake at 300° for 30 to 40 minutes. Cool, cut into squares, and top with Jack Daniel's Caramel Sauce and whipped cream, if desired.
Yield: 8 servings.

Chocolate Chess Squares with Jack Daniel's Caramel Sauce

This recipe was introduced during the time Louise Gregory was preparing the desserts. Guest have always given it rave reviews!

½ cup butter
2 squares unsweetened chocolate
¼ cup all-purpose flour
2 eggs, slightly beaten
1 cup sugar
½ cup pecans, chopped
1 teaspoon vanilla extract
Jack Daniel's Caramel Sauce (this page)

In a saucepan combine the butter and chocolate. Melt over low heat and set aside. In a medium bowl mix the flour, eggs, sugar, nuts, and vanilla. Add the egg mixture to the chocolate mixture. Pour into a well-greased 8-inch square pan. Bake at 350° for 20 to 25 minutes. Cool. To serve, cut into squares and top with Jack Daniel's Caramel Sauce and a dollop of whipped cream.
Yield: 9 servings.

Portrait of a Great Lady

Miss Mary Bobo left her imprint on her community with her friendship, integrity, and personality. She left a larger imprint on the community at large by the quality of her establishment, the enduring fame of her hospitality, and the wonderful foods that guests have enjoyed at her table since 1908. Miss Mary continues to be remembered and revered as a lady of virtue and character, something we all would do well to emulate.

Jack Daniel's Dessert Sauce

1 cup sugar
½ cup buttermilk
1 tablespoon butter
1 tablespoon light corn syrup
¼ teaspoon baking soda
1 tablespoon Jack Daniel's Whiskey

In a saucepan combine the sugar, butter-milk, butter, and corn syrup over medium heat. Bring the mixture to a boil. Boil for 5 to 7 minutes. Remove the pan from the heat. Add the baking soda, but do not stir. Cool to warm, then add the Jack Daniel's Whiskey and stir. Serve at room temperature over Applesauce Cake (see page 127), or it's delicious spooned over apple pie.
Yield: 1½ cups.

Crowning Glory Sauce

1 cup sugar
½ cup butter
½ cup half-and-half
¼ teaspoon cinnamon
Dash nutmeg
¼ cup Jack Daniel's Whiskey

In a skillet melt the sugar over medium heat until light brown in color. Remove from the heat and cool slightly. Add the butter and stir until combined. Stir in the remaining ingredients and cook until thickened. This is delicious over ice cream, pound cake, or bread pudding.
Yield: 1½ cups.

Custard Sauce Topping

2 cups whipping cream
⅔ cups milk
1 vanilla bean
6 egg yolks
⅔ cup sugar
Pinch of salt

In a saucepan combine the cream and milk. Split the vanilla bean, scrape the seeds into the milk, and add the bean. Bring the mixture to a boil. Remove the pan from the heat, cover the pan, and let it rest for 40 minutes to allow the flavors to meld.

In a medium mixing bowl beat the egg yolks. Add the sugar and salt and blend well. Return the cream to the stove and bring it to a boil again. Stir a small amount of the hot milk into the egg mixture, then gradually add all of the egg mixture to the cream, stir-ring constantly over low heat, being careful not to boil again. The custard will thicken and coat the spoon in about 4 minutes. Strain the custard into a bowl, removing the vanilla bean and seeds. Cover and refrigerate for at least 2 hours before serving.

This also is a wonderful topping for pound cake, puddings, or tarts.
Yield: 3 cups.

Uncle Jack's Fondue

1 pound semisweet chocolate
½ cup heavy cream
¼ cup Jack Daniel's Whiskey

In a saucepan or fondue pot melt the choco-late. Add the cream and Jack Daniel's Whiskey. Stir until smooth. Use as a dip for fruit or coffee cake.

Miss Mary's Chocolate Sauce for Ice Cream

2 tablespoons cocoa
1 cup sugar
⅔ cup milk
Pinch salt

In a saucepan mix the cocoa and sugar with enough water to let the sugar melt. Simmer over low heat. Let the syrup cool. Add the milk and salt, and then bring the sauce to a boil. Boil for 10 minutes. Remove the pan from the heat and let the sauce cool.

Serve hot or cold. Will keep in refrigerator several days.
Yield: 1½ cups.

Lynchburg's Famous Sauce

2 cups sugar
3 tablespoons all-purpose flour
2 cups milk
½ cup butter
Pinch of salt
Jack Daniel's Whiskey

In a saucepan combine the sugar and flour. Add the milk, butter, and salt. Cook over medium heat until thick, stirring contantly. Remove the pan from the heat and add Jack Daniel's Whiskey to taste. Serve over bread pudding or plain cake.
Yield: 3 cups.

Conclusion:
Miss Bobo's at Eventide

Evening time at Miss Mary Bobo's Boarding House is just about the same today as it was earlier this century. Shops close early on the square; there are no late evenings or nine o'clock store closings here in Lynchburg. Shopkeepers lock their doors, and folks go home to cook supper. Some stroll up the street past the big house that sits slightly off-center between the two huge sugar maple trees. The white picket fence with no gate marks the property just a slight half-block off the square. The front porch today is probably missing the porch sitters of just a few decades back, but the cooks *just possibly* are in the kitchen, cooking up something wonderful for the occasional evening events that still warm this old house. If it is summertime, the *happening* just might be a wedding reception or rehearsal dinner. The bride's mother might be placing bowls of roses with ribbons and grape ivy streamers along the big tables and placing little vases of violets with lace at each dinner plate. The aroma of Miss Mary's Famous Chicken and Pastry, hot rolls, or a fresh-baked Tennessee Whiskey Cake fills the house and the surrounding porches and yard because the doors and windows are open wide to the cool evening air.

If it is holiday time, then the house is closed and warm with the ovens baking Tennessee Country Ham and Baked Chicken and Dressing. The fragrant Tipsy Sweet Potatoes and Dew Drop Biscuits fill the air with promises of the feast to come. A grand old cedar tree stands in the parlor decorated with country ornaments and colored lights, and the antique music box has been wound and is filling the house with the musical charm of centuries. The tables and mantles and outside doors are strung with garlands and wreaths of evergreen adorned with large red bows. The wooden reindeer stand alert in the front yard to greet each guest as they briskly move from car to house.

Up the street the town's magnificent Christmas tree is aglow with lights in the Gazebo Park on the Square. The lights that line the stores make Lynchburg seem very "uptown," but the stores themselves prove differently. They are dark and locked. Folks have gone home for their own family feast, perhaps a cup of boiled custard with a bit of the hometown product to flavor it. Even the rush of holiday shopping and bustle of holiday preparations haven't changed this little town.

Have we stepped back in time? Maybe, just maybe, we have found a place that the busy world overlooked in a headlong race to *get somewhere.*

Miss Bobo worked for many years, and she worked to make her boarding house a success. People today want to retire young, to eat well, and take life easy. By today's standards this is *rich*. It just might be that Miss Mary had a secret in working into old age, still eating hearty midday meals, and living at a pace of life almost forgotten today. Is this what contributed to her longevity? And what about contentment? These are thoughts to contemplate while sitting on a front porch. The porch at Miss Mary Bobo's Boarding House is empty. All we need is a tall glass of iced tea and a plate of Front Porch Crackers. There is nothing to interrupt our thoughts, except perhaps an occasional "Howdy!" or "Evenin'" from the neighbors passing by.

Index